Prehistoric
NEW ZEALAND

Contents

A note on the reconstructions

These reconstructions attempt to present a picture of New Zealand as it may have appeared at different stages in its history. They have been worked on stretched fabriano hot-pressed paper in a mixture of gouache, watercolour and pencil. They are images which have been developed after much preliminary consultation, discussion and research, and as such are a combination of scientific fact and necessary imaginative reconstruction.

As each work developed, problems peculiar to them developed. In the Jurassic reconstruction, for example, the individual species — *Paryphanta busbyi, Peripatus, Hemideina megacephala, Leiopelma hochstetteri* — are presented as they exist today; ancestors of these species are known to have existed in the Jurassic although not necessarily in the form depicted. The appearance of the ancestral ratite is purely speculative. Lacking any adequate fossil record, the appearance of such a species can only be based on informed scientific supposition.

Elsewhere, photographic sources have been used extensively, being especially appropriate, for example, in the Taupo eruption reconstruction where photographic records of the recent Mt St Helens eruption were the primary pictorial source used.

The role of the artist is to present the maximum amount of visual information in a manner which is interesting but not incongruous. The association between different species depicted, for example in the postglacial bird reconstruction, is the association of time rather than habitat — the intention here is to demonstrate the existence of different species at a particular time. The requirement that each picture convey as much information as possible leads to the device of placing the individual species in a proximity, which probably did not actually occur.

I would like to acknowledge the advice and support of the following: Jack Grant-Mackie, Graeme Stevens, Beverley McCulloch, Richard Holdaway, Phillip Ridge, Steve Henderson, Mike Bradstock, Alvin Smith, Joan Wiffen, my family, and especially my children, Cathlin and Miriam.

The following are some of the references used in the individual reconstructions:
Cambrian sea (pp.18-19): Stevens, G. R., *Lands in Collision*, DSIR Information Series 161, Wellington, 1985; Stevens, G. R., *New Zealand Adrift*, A. H. & A. W. Reed, Wellington, 1980.
Jurassic migrants (pp. 36-37): Attenborough, D., *Discovering Life on Earth*, Collins, London, 1981; Barnett, S., *New Zealand in the Wild*, Collins, Auckland, 1985; Burian, Z., *Prehistoric Animals and Plants*, Hamlyn, London, 1979; Molloy, L., *The Ancient Islands*, Port Nicholson Press, Wellington, 1982; Powell, A. W. B., *Native Animals of New Zealand*, Auckland Museum, 1975; Scherell, R., *The Tuatara, Lizards and Frogs of New Zealand*, Collins, Auckland, 1966; Stevens, G. R., *Lands in Collision*, DSIR, Wellington, 1985; Stewart, W. N., *Palaeobotany and the Evolution of Plants*, Cambridge University Press, Cambridge, 1983; White, M., *The Greening of Gondwana*, Reed, Sydney, 1986; *Forest and Bird*, Vol. 154, No. 3, August 1984; Vol 17, No. 4, November 1986.
Postglacial birds (pp. 100-101): Hoskings, E., *Eric Hosking's Birds*, Pelham, London, 1979; Moon, G., *The Birds Around Us*, Heinemann, Auckland, 1979; Serventy, V., *The Desert Sea*, Macmillan, Melbourne, 1985; Temple, P. and C. Gaskin, *Moa*, Collins, Auckland, 1985; *Forest and Bird*, Vol. 15, No. 2, May 1984; Vol. 17, No. 4, November 1986.
Taupo eruption (pp. 106-7): Pascoe, J., *National Parks of New Zealand*, Government Printer, Wellington, 1974; *National Geographic*, Vol. 159, No. 1; Vol. 160, No. 6; Vol. 162, No. 5.
Moas (pp. 116-17): Barnett, S., (ed.), *New Zealand in the Wild*, Collins, Auckland, 1985; Temple, P. and C. Gaskin, *Moa*, Collins, Auckland, 1985; Johns J. and C. Chavesse, *Forest World of New Zealand*, Reed, Wellington, 1975; Moon, G., *The Birds Around Us*, Heinemann, Auckland, 1979.

Vivian Ward

The reconstructions on pp.48-9 (**New Zealand dinosaurs**) and on pp.56-7 (**Mesozoic marine reptiles**) are by Geoffrey Cox and are reproduced here by permission of NZ Post and HarperCollins*Publishers* respectively. The New Zealand dinosaurs reconstruction was first published in *Stamp of the Dinosaur* (NZ Post), and that of the marine reptiles in *Prehistoric Animals of New Zealand* (HarperCollins*Publishers*).

The following are references used by Geoffrey Cox in painting these illustrations:
New Zealand dinosaurs (pp. 48-50): Czerkas, S. and G. Czerkas, *Dinosaurs: A Global View*, Dragon's World, Limpsfield, Surrey, 1990; Czerkas, S. and C. Olsen (eds), *Dinosaurs Past and Present*, Vols I & II, Natural History Museum of Los Angeles County/University of Washington Press, Seattle and London, 1987; Dobson, P., (ed.), *Encyclopedia of Dinosaurs*, Publications International Ltd, Lincolnwood, Illinois, 1990; Paul, G., *Predatory Dinosaurs of the World*, New York Academy of Sciences, Simon & Schuster Inc., New York, 1989.
Mesozoic marine reptiles (pp. 56-7): Augusta, J. and Z. Burian, *Prehistoric Animals,* Spring Books, London, 1955; Benes, J. and Z. Burian, *Prehistoric Animals and Plants*, Hamlyn, London, 1979; Spinar, Z. and Z. Burian, *Life Before Man*, Thames and Hudson, London, 1972; *Dinosaurs and their Living Relatives*, British Museum/Cambridge University Press, Cambridge, 1979.

Photographic credits
The editors of *Prehistoric New Zealand* are indebted to the following photographers and institutions for their invaluable assistance:
Andris Apse Ltd: frontispiece, pp. 68-9, 88-9, 102-103; **British Museum:** p. 114; **Canterbury Museum:** p.113; **Brian Chudleigh:** p. 99; **John Fennell** (JF): pp. 14, 20, 21, 26, 45, 51, 54 (left), 58, 72; **Henk Haazen** (HH): pp.62-3, 63, 83; **Lloyd Homer** (New Zealand Geological Survey): pp. 42-3; **Matt McGlone:** pp. 47 (right), 95, 108, 109; **Brian Molloy:** pp. 91, 94; **Rod Morris** (RM): pp. 10, 11, 24, 25, 30, 31, 34, 34-5, 35, 38 (below left and right), 44, 46, 54 (below), 55, 61, 64, 70, 72-3, 73, 74, 75 (right), 80, 80-1, 84, 84-5, 87 (insets), 90, 97, 98, 99 (above), 112 (above), 115, 120, 121; **G. R. (Dick) Roberts** (GR): pp. 11, 19, 22, 30, 38 (bottom right), 47, (above), 74-5 (above right), 78, 78-9, 79, 81, 85, 87 (full page), 90, 93, 94-5, 109, 124; **Michael Trotter:** p. 112 (left); **Waihi Museum:** pp. 122-23; **John Warham:** p. 67; **Joan Wiffen:** p. 50; **Wilson & Horton Ltd:** pp. 76, 104, 118.

Introduction

In the last 20 years our understanding of the earth has been revolutionised by a startling new concept called plate tectonics. By uniting previously disparate disciplines, it has illuminated hitherto unexplained aspects of our planet. The riddles of our own prehistory can now be solved.

FROM the beginnings of European exploration of New Zealand, it was realised that here was a peculiarly unique country. As the natural history collections obtained by the various early explorers were examined and interpreted, the special character of much of the New Zealand fauna and flora became apparent. Later, animals such as the kiwi, moa, takahe and the tuatara were the subject of much attention from scientists and the general public alike and leading European naturalists took part in the scientific description of New Zealand species.

What so intrigued the early explorers and naturalists was the absence of the large land mammals that are so much a feature of life elsewhere in the world. What is more, no large land mammals had ever existed here. Instead, New Zealand was the home of a prolific array of ancient forms of life. The concept was staggering, and it is quaint to reflect now how in some of the early writings New Zealand was likened to a lost Arcadia, the Garden of Eden before the Fall. Nevertheless, it was soon realised that New Zealand must have been isolated before the appearance of advanced predatory animal life. At that time it was believed that the world's continents were somehow locked into position and initially scientists speculated that New Zealand had only become isolated when the 'land bridges' that had formerly linked New Zealand to its continental neighbours had submerged. These connections, or 'bridges', while originally providing routes for early animals and plants to move into New Zealand in the distant past, were believed to have sunk without trace beneath the oceans, like some lost Atlantis, denying access to the more advanced animal life of later geological times.

With the improvement of geological knowledge, and as technological advances made it possible to explore and chart the ocean floor in a systematic way, it became clear that the sea floor was not a graveyard of sunken and dismembered land bridges that when emergent in the past may have linked New Zealand to neighbouring continents. Instead, the oceanic explorations revealed the presence of vast areas of oceanic rocks that not by any stretch of imagination could possibly have been continental. This discovery in the New Zealand area and elsewhere in the world paved the way for the acceptance of the theory of continental drift and its modern version, plate tectonics.

New ways of thinking about the earth

The earth sciences are now in the midst of a new flowering — a golden age of an unprecedented uniting and synthesis of many hitherto unexplained, or inadequately explained, aspects of our planet. Seemingly isolated topics of both geology and geophysics have taken on new patterns and are now seen as contributing parts of a unifying conceptual framework known as plate tectonics. For many years the earth sciences were fragmented and pigeonholed. There were compartments for the study of strata, volcanic rocks and igneous bodies (that is, once-molten rocks) such as granite. Other compartments dealt with the structure and shape of the land. Palaeontology, the study of fossils, seemed to be endless lists of unpronounceable and mysterious names. Earthquakes and volcanoes were exciting, but were off in a corner by themselves. How all these phenomena were related was cloaked in obscurity. Plate tectonics and its predecessor continental drift have, however, provided a central theme, linking the whole spectrum of geological observations.

Plate tectonics views the exterior of the earth as an ever-changing mobile surface. The earth's rocky outer layer or lithosphere (i.e. 'rock-sphere') is broken into huge interlocking plate-like segments that are commonly thousands of kilometres across but, as we know from earthquake data, are only about 100 kilometres thick. These plates are all moving in relation to one another, like giant ice floes jostling one another on the surface of some vast polar sea. In some places the plates are being jammed together so that they collide and over-ride each other. Such plate collisions have crumpled the converging plate margins like a wrinkled rug, creating huge chains of folded mountains such as the Himalayas. Plates may also slide past one another, creating enormous zones of cracked, crushed and shattered rock. In other places the earth's lithosphere is being torn apart along enormous fracture lines or rift zones, zig-zagging across the surface of the earth, to give it an appearance similar to that of seams on the surface of a giant cricket ball. Most of these rift zones cross the ocean floors, where they form gigantic globe-encircling lines of submarine mountains. Where they traverse the land they form rift valleys, like those of East Africa, and provide the foci for intense earthquake and volcanic activity. The splitting that takes place along the rift zones has the effect of reducing pressures within the earth, leading to melting in the dense, hot iron and magnesium-rich silicate rocks of the mantle.

At the same time as the earth's surface splits and moves apart, molten material is injected upwards into the rift zone, creating a narrow band of new crust all along the centre of the rift like newly formed scar tissue. As the earth's surface continues to stretch and split, this process is repeated, each eruption of molten material splitting the preceding injection of rock into two strips and wedging aside the strips so that they are progressively shunted away from the actual line of the rift. Eventually, strips of rock identical in age and composition, and originating from the same source, are separated by thousands of kilometres.

Over millions of years new areas of crust have been created, new oceans formed and existing oceans widened. The continual creation of new sea floor along the rift zones or 'spread centres' is termed sea-floor spreading and the process can be likened to that of a moving conveyor belt, with the continents being carried passively along the belt. Yet, such inexorable expansion of the sea floor cannot go on forever, otherwise the oceans and indeed our planet itself would get larger and larger. So, where does the expanding sea floor go? The deep sea trenches of the world are thought to hold the answer to this riddle. They are regarded as the areas in the crust where old sea floor is being actively consumed in 'subduction zones'. The sea floor, riding on the conveyor belt of sea-floor spreading, arrives at an oceanic trench where it is over-ridden and sinks, sliding obliquely deeper and deeper into the underlying mantle. As it does, the enormous frictional forces involved in the downthrusting process generate innumerable earthquakes. These earthquakes can be traced downwards into the earth as a sloping zone (the Benioff Zone), extending to depths of 600–700 kilometres.

The earthquake swarms of the Benioff Zone define the upper surface of the descending slab of sea floor. As the slab descends further and further down into the mantle it enters into progressively hotter regions until it begins to melt. Also dragged down with the sea floor slab are large parts of the covering layers of sediment, much of them derived from adjacent continents and hence of continental composition. As melting occurs, molten rock (magma) forms, containing a mixture of both sea floor and continental rocks. The magma finds its way to the surface, there to erupt on both land and sea. There is, therefore, a close association between subduction zones and volcanic activity.

The general picture is that the sea floor created at the spreading ridges is being swallowed up along subduction zones marked by submarine trenches, volcanic activity and earthquake zones concentrated along downward-dipping Benioff Zones.

The plate tectonic view of the earth differs from that of the earlier continental drift theory in several important respects. Although the interiors (cores or nucleii) of the continents are indeed old, as most earlier geologists believed, on the other hand, the oceans are young, and not ancient features of the earth as previously thought. Now, the continents are not seen to be 'drifting' as independent entities. Rather, they are seen to be carried,

The earth's crust is composed of at least 15 rigid plates of lithosphere, and almost all the earthquake, volcanic and mountain-building activity takes place along their boundaries. New Zealand straddles one such active zone, astride the boundary between the Indian-Australian and Pacific Plates.

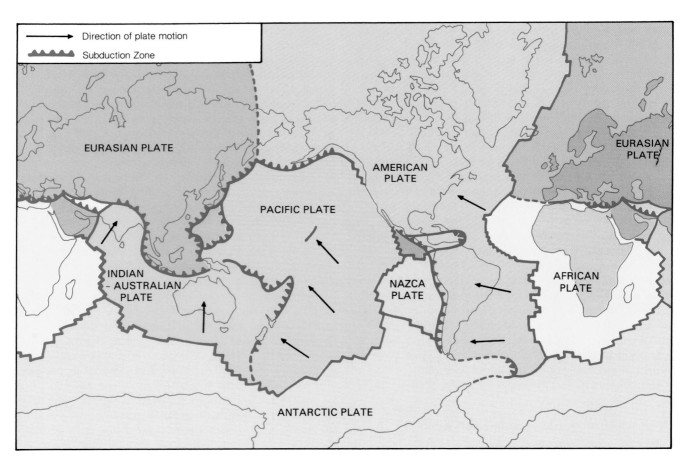

Direction of plate motion
Subduction Zone

EURASIAN PLATE

EURASIAN PLATE

AMERICAN PLATE

PACIFIC PLATE

INDIAN - AUSTRALIAN PLATE

NAZCA PLATE

AFRICAN PLATE

ANTARCTIC PLATE

almost as passengers, on the surface of composite plates, 100 kilometres or so thick. The plates glide over a zone of hot weak rock called the 'asthenosphere' (or weak sphere), situated some 100 kilometres down in the upper mantle.

Mapping of the earth has shown that the earth's outer surface is composed of at least 15 interlocking plates of various sizes. Seven plates are particularly large and occupy considerable areas of the globe. The Pacific Plate, for example, underlies most of the Pacific Ocean. Other smaller plates are of regional rather than global extent: for example, the Juan de Fuca Plate includes a small segment of crust flanking the west coast of North America. Still smaller 'micro-plates' or 'terranes' can also be recognised as fragments or chips that have been broken off larger plates in the past and have since been moving independently.

Except for the Pacific Plate, the major plates include both relatively old, light, high-standing continental crust and younger, heavier, lower-standing oceanic crust, as well as part of the upper mantle beneath. The Pacific Plate and several smaller ones are almost wholly oceanic, while the crustal parts of a few small plates and terranes are mainly or wholly continental.

The boundaries between individual plates can be classified into four principal types. Divergent or spreading boundaries are developed where plates are separating and new material is being added by the upwelling of molten rock. Convergent boundaries are developed where plates converge and one plate is over-ridden and descends into the mantle, there to be consumed in a subduction zone. Collision boundaries are developed where continents riding on plates have collided along former subduction zones and have become 'welded' together to form 'suture' zones of folded mountain ranges. Transform fault boundaries are developed in instances where although two plates are touching there are none of the effects of a bruising contact, but rather the plates simply glide past one another along a major boundary fault line, without the addition or destruction of plate material. Most, but not all, of the earth's restless activity is concentrated along the plate boundaries — earthquakes, volcanoes, mountain-building, deep sea trenches, deep melting and ore deposits.

The making of New Zealand

Where, then, does New Zealand fit into the global plate tectonic picture? Although we know very little about how exactly the earth's plates were arranged in the past, we do know that New Zealand was part of a vast supercontinent called Gondwana up to the time the Tasman Sea began to form between about 80 and 60 million years ago. For most of this time the site of modern New Zealand was an area on the ocean floor on the eastern edge of Gondwana, flanked by eastern Australia, Tasmania and Antarctica.

Deep sea-floor drilling in the last 20 years has revealed that new sea-floor is being continually created along the rift zones of plate margins.

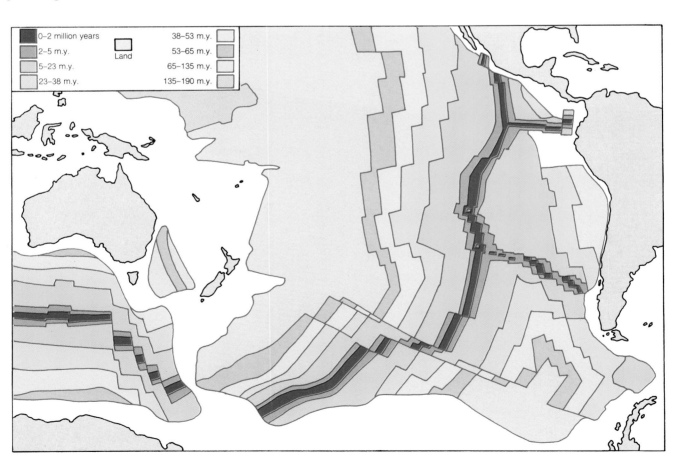

In other words, for much of its early history no large identifiable landmass has been present in the New Zealand region. At times archipelagoes and scattered islands of volcanic origin have come into existence, only to be eroded away. The problem, then, is in defining exactly what is New Zealand. The shape of the New Zealand landmass as we know it is a very recent feature and only came into existence some 10,000 years ago. Like the proverbial pocketknife with three new blades and two new handles, our land has undergone many changes and has had a great variety of shapes and sizes in the past. Around 140 million years ago, during a period we now term the mid-Mesozoic Era, an ancestral landmass was, however, created in the New Zealand region. And what a land! It extended northwards to at least New Caledonia, southwards to the edge of the Campbell Plateau (south of the Campbell and Auckland Islands), westwards to the Australian continent and eastwards to the Chathams. The geologic processes that fashioned this ancestral landmass were complex and will be discussed in greater depth later (see pages 32–33). At this stage, all we need to say is that as far as we can tell, throughout virtually its entire existence New Zealand has not been very far away from the activity associated with a convergent plate margin. During the Mesozoic the floor of the ancestral Pacific was being progressively thrust under the eastern edge of Gondwana, along a zone of subduction. For millions of years more and more sea floor was being conveyed to and consumed in the subduction zone. Eventually, a mass of sediment, originally deposited off the coast of West Antarctica and Australia, arrived at the subduction zone and, being buoyant continental material, could not be consumed in the subduction zone. Instead, it was thrust into contact with the sediments that had accumulated in the submarine trench and on the flanks of the volcanic arc. The immense shearing and buckling movements that resulted broke the sea floor and upper mantle into slices that were caught up and thrust into the contorted piles of sediment. The resulting twisted and deformed mass was pushed up to form land. These major earth movements, grouped together as the Rangitata Orogeny or mountain-building phase, are thought to have occurred mainly during the late Jurassic and early Cretaceous (140–120 million years ago) and the ancestral land created in this way was the first sizeable landmass to exist in the New Zealand area.

As we've mentioned, the edges of this ancestral new land virtually nudged the edges of both Antarctica and Australia. Here, at last, were the 'lost land bridges' that had so preoccupied and fascinated the early scientists. It was not necessary, however, to have continuous land to form a 'bridge'. Rather, strings of closely spaced islands, like those of eastern Indonesia today, may have provided a perfectly adequate route for many land plants and creatures. Many land animals can survive lengthy voyages on floating trees, in the aftermath of a storm, and some, if they have to, can swim considerable distances. From Gondwana, vibrant tides of plant and animal species now swept across the newly formed land, filling its recesses, creating their own ecological niches. It was during this time that many of the species we now regard as endemic or unique to New Zealand migrated here. Ancestors of the tuatara, moa, kiwi, weta, the New Zealand frog, as well as the ancestral podocarps (now

RM

represented in the New Zealand forest by such trees as totara, miro, matai, kahikatea, rimu etc.) arrived during this time.

This landmass persisted until the end of the Mesozoic, gradually weathering and eroding away. And then between 80–65 million years ago, at the close of the Mesozoic, sea-floor spreading began between ancestral New Zealand and Australia, and the embryonic Tasman Sea came into being. Whereas New Zealand had once been linked to Australia, now it was isolated by a narrow band of sea. Denied these land links, New Zealand would not share in the subsequent evolution of the monotremes and marsupials that are such a feature of Australia's unique fauna. No platypus or koala would roam our shores.

Isolated from Australia, New Zealand was, nevertheless, still tentatively linked to Antarctica, although by now the ancestral landmass had eroded to such an extent that it was but a rump of its former self. And then about 55 million years ago, the focus of sea-floor spreading shifted to between Australia and Antarctica. As a result, these two lands that up to then had been in close contact, started to move apart, forming the Southern Ocean. New Zealand now became fixed in relation to Australia. In other words, both Australia and New Zealand became part of the Indian-Australian Plate, and as that plate pulled away from the Antarctic Plate and drifted northwards so did New Zealand. Our isolation complete, we would not witness the evolution and flourishing of the Class Mammalia and that most capricious of its species, *Homo sapiens*.

*   *   *

Today New Zealand straddles the boundary between the Pacific and Indian-Australian plates. To the north of New Zealand the structure of the plate boundary is reasonably straight-forward. The Pacific Ocean floor is being subducted under the edge of the Indian-Australian Plate. This is accompanied by the development of a submarine trench, Benioff Zone, volcanic island arc etc. (the Tonga-Kermadec-Hikurangi trench system).

A similar plate boundary structure exists to the south of New Zealand (the Macquarie system). However, along this boundary the edge of the Pacific Plate is being pushed *over* the Indian-Australian Plate, so that all the features associated with subduction are developed as a mirror-image of the Tonga-Kermadec-Hikurangi system dying out under the northern part of the South Island, and the Macquarie system dying out as it approaches Fiordland.

As may be expected, the geology of New Zealand reflects the complexities of being the go-between for the two systems: having been squeezed, pushed, pulled and eventually torn apart. The axial ranges which form the backbone of the modern country are a visible link between the two subduction systems. Throughout its long geological history New Zealand has played a variety of roles, but has never been very far away from an active plate margin.

The future of New Zealand, geologically speaking, is difficult to foretell. If the boundary between the Indian-Australian Plate and the Pacific Plate remains in its present position, virtually bisecting the country, and if the Indian-Australian Plate continues to move away from the Antarctic Plate (a process that started about 55 million years ago), New Zealand may at some stage in the future

LEFT: *Pohutukawa forest, Poor Knights Islands. The ancestor of the pohutukawa came to New Zealand some time in the Paleocene, 65–53 million years ago.* BELOW: *A bull sea-elephant. Apart from three species of bats, New Zealand's only endemic mammals are the marine mammals — sea-elephants, sea lions and seals — whose ancestors probably came to New Zealand during the Miocene, 24–5 million years ago.* RIGHT: *The tree ferns, so characteristic of New Zealand's forests, are of archaic varieties that came to the south-west Pacific in the early Mesozoic, more than 190 million years ago.*

RM

GR

find itself as two groups of islands. In this scenario the part of New Zealand west of the Alpine Fault is carried northwards as part of the Indian-Australian Plate, leaving the part of New Zealand east of the Alpine Fault sitting on the edge of the Pacific Plate.

An alternative scenario views the present New Zealand geological situation as being transitional. In this view the situation has been complicated by the arrival at the plate edge of that part of New Zealand now lying east of the Alpine Fault. Because it is continental, and therefore buoyant, this segment of land will probably not go down the Tonga-Kermadec-Hikurangi trench. If this is so, the scene may be set for a side-stepping movement of the plate boundary eastwards, out into the Pacific. If this happens, all of the New Zealand landmass will drift steadily northwards as part of the Indian-Australian Plate, and 20 million years into the future New Zealanders will be basking in tropical sunshine!

The succession of animal life

Before humans arrived on the scene about 1,000 years ago, New Zealand was a land with a very 'unbalanced' flora and fauna. Many plant and animal groups, widespread elsewhere in the world, were absent from primaeval New Zealand. As we now know, this was because New Zealand had been cut off from the rest of the world during the development of these animals and plants.

By piecing together the fragmentary fossil record preserved in the rocks we have been able to establish an 'order of succession', or chronology, of animal and plant life. We can, for example, recognise an age of 'ancient life' or 'Palaeozoic' (*palaios* = ancient), when most animals and plants were of ancient and often bizarre type. Then we can establish an age of 'middle life' or 'Mesozoic' (*mesos* = middle), midway between the old and the new. Then finally we have an age of 'recent life' (Cenozoic, sometimes spelled Kainozoic or Cainozoic, derived from the Greek *kainos* or *cenos* meaning recent), during which we see the progressive appearance of animals and plants that can be recognised immediately as being like modern creatures. Within these three broad eras there are further, more discrete, categories.

As we go back through geological time, we can trace, through the study of fossil life, a steady progression of animals and plants. As time passed the original flora and fauna living in a particular area were progressively replaced by more advanced forms. In the animal kingdom, for example, we see an overall progression from life in the sea to life on the land. The sea provided a cosy, almost insulated, environment, whereas the land, with its variety of often harsh habitats, represented a great challenge to the early animals. As far as we know, before about 390 million years ago, much of the development in the animal kingdom took place in the sea. From simple organisms, various fish types evolved, many of which lived in New Zealand waters. And then in the Devonian,

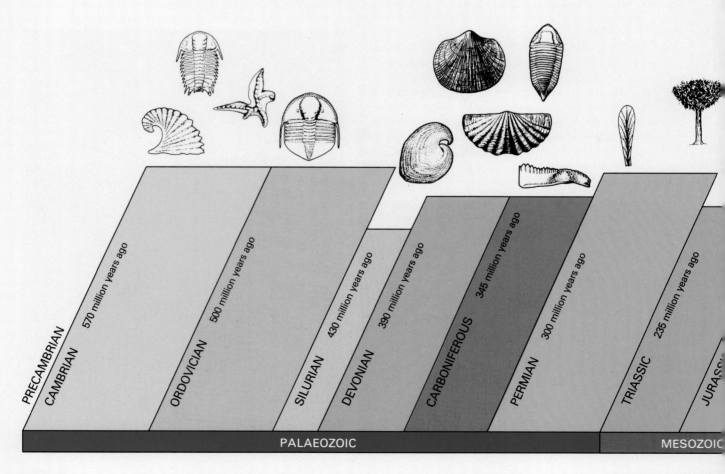

PRECAMBRIAN | CAMBRIAN 570 million years ago | ORDOVICIAN 500 million years ago | SILURIAN 430 million years ago | DEVONIAN 390 million years ago | CARBONIFEROUS 345 million years ago | PERMIAN 300 million years ago | TRIASSIC 235 million years ago | JURASSIC

PALAEOZOIC   MESOZOIC

390–345 million years ago, fish appeared with stout fleshy fins, capable of developing into legs. This led to the eventual development of the amphibians, animals able to live on both land and water, but still dependent on water for their reproductive cycle.

A factor that undoubtedly influenced the evolution of fish that could live out of the water was that, to judge from fossil records, these fish populated lakes and rivers subject to periodic droughts. It was probably this inhospitable environment that forced certain individuals within each species to crawl in search of water.

The reptiles that first appeared some 300 million years ago, and presumably evolved from amphibians, were the first animals to cut the ties to the water, and could freely live and reproduce on the land. The reptiles were covered with massively thickened scales, developed from those of their fish and amphibian ancestors, to protect them from predators, but also to insulate them from the rigours of the terrestrial environment. They were cold-blooded and although their scaly covering did help to conserve bodily heat their activity was governed by the temperature of the environment. Cool temperatures would slow them down so that they were capable of only sluggish movements.

The reptiles had their heyday in the Mesozoic Era (235–65) million years ago) and in many countries, including New Zealand, dinosaurs roamed the land. Some reptiles developed paddle-like limbs and a streamlined shape and returned to the sea. Other reptiles developed large sail-like flaps of skin extending between their greatly elongated fingers and their sides. These could glide in the air, but it is doubtful whether they could actually fly by flapping their wings. Some reptiles, however, formed feathers from their reptilian scales, and developed light hollow bones and a large keel-like chest bone to provide attachment for powerful wing muscles. These feathered reptiles, with scale-clad legs (still present in modern birds, as a hint of their reptilian ancestry), reptilian teeth and clawed wings (both lost in modern birds), first appeared in the late Jurassic, about 150–140 million years ago.

By Jurassic times, therefore, amphibians and reptiles were roaming the land and the first birds had just evolved from reptilian stock. When the ancestral New Zealand landmass came into being during this time, it was these animals that migrated here. The most important thing to remember, however, is that this period represents the one and only time in our entire history when optimal conditions existed for land animals to walk or island-hop to New Zealand. The sad thing is that we have very little record of past land life in New Zealand — such are the vagaries of fossil preservation.

The chances of fossil preservation

If creatures are living in the sea, the chances are fairly good that eventually they will be preserved in some way or other. A sea creature when it dies sinks to the bottom and starts to decay. If this creature has landed in an area

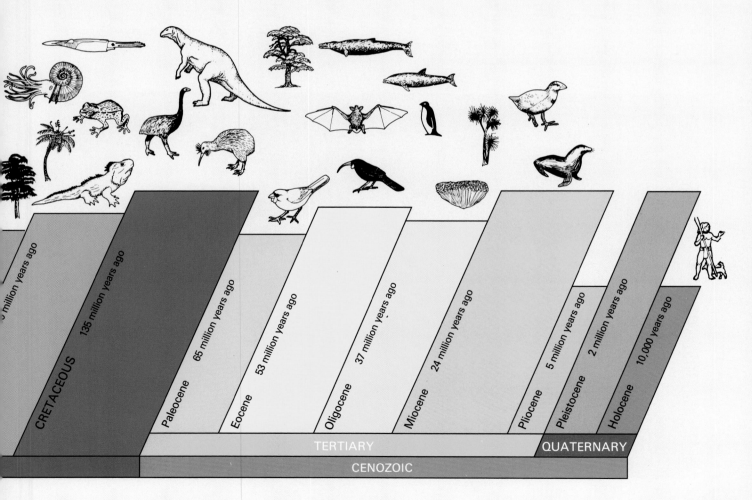

million years ago | 135 million years ago | 65 million years ago | 53 million years ago | 37 million years ago | 24 million years ago | 5 million years ago | 2 million years ago | 10,000 years ago

CRETACEOUS | Paleocene | Eocene | Oligocene | Miocene | Pliocene | Pleistocene | Holocene

TERTIARY   QUATERNARY

CENOZOIC

in which muds and sands are accumulating at a rapid rate, it is quickly buried and, as the various bacteria and fungi causing decomposition require oxygen, burial puts an immediate stop to decay and the creature is preserved in entirety. If, however, the dead creature lies on the sea floor for some time, scavengers may consume it or break it into pieces. Alternatively, if decay runs its full course, the creature's flesh is reduced to a soft pulp that is eventually winnowed away by currents. Only the hard parts of the body remain and these may also disintegrate under the attack of acids and alkalis generated as by-products of the decay process. The disarticulated hard parts, if they survive, may, however, be eventually buried and thus preserved.

In time the ocean-floor sediments are raised above sea level to form land, rivers and streams cut gorges, and, if we are lucky, geologists will come along and find the preserved creatures — often now 'petrified' by the addition of various minerals that soaked into every pore and crevice of the creature's body.

Although the preservation of marine creatures is a chancy business, the dice are even more loaded against land creatures. If, for instance, a cow dies out in a paddock, decay rapidly sets in and the body begins to disintegrate. Scavengers may hasten the disintegration. Very soon all that is left are some sunbleached bones lying scattered on the surface, and in time even these will decay, under the combined effects of sunlight's ultraviolet rays, acidic rain and the various natural acids and alkalis in the soil. Often very soon nothing is left.

All in all, the chances are not very good of preserving a sample of the land creatures that lived in an area at any particular time. At times in the past dinosaurs and moas have been preserved in ancient lake, swamp or river deposits. Also, creatures have sometimes fallen down pot-holes or other cracks in the earth and have been preserved. Others have been preserved in caves. Compared with the chances of preservation in the marine environment, however, these types of preservation require special circumstances. Large parts of North America, for example, were swampy river plains at the time (Jurassic and Cretaceous) when ancestral New Zealand was created. Meandering rivers, continually shifting, formed large areas of quicksand and swamps, suitable for trapping many of the huge dinosaurs that roamed the land at that time. Many animals were thus preserved in deposits on the land, and, as little erosion or earth movement has occurred since then, the deposits are still in their original position.

The ancestral New Zealand land undoubtedly had creatures roaming its surface and many were probably preserved in river, swamp and lake deposits. As we will see, this primaeval land was gradually whittled away by rivers, streams and the sea, so that by about 30 million years ago most of it was back below the ocean again. Thus, any land deposits dating back to the Mesozoic and early Cenozoic have probably been destroyed.

The major point of all this is that while areas like central North America, with a long history of earth stability, have a rich record of land life, going back to the Mesozoic and beyond, New Zealand, going up and down like a yo-yo, has a very poor land record. However, by using information from other countries with good records of fossil land life, and from pollen analysis (to give us an idea of the vegetation), we have been able to build up a picture, albeit rather sketchy, of the past.

It remains to portray that somewhat incomplete picture.

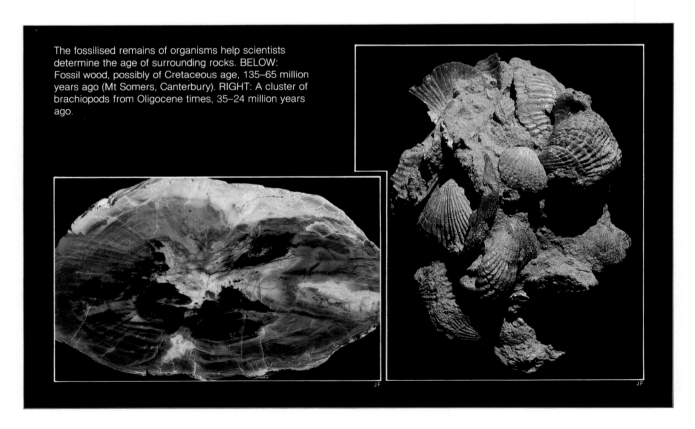

The fossilised remains of organisms help scientists determine the age of surrounding rocks. BELOW: Fossil wood, possibly of Cretaceous age, 135–65 million years ago (Mt Somers, Canterbury). RIGHT: A cluster of brachiopods from Oligocene times, 35–24 million years ago.

1. Gondwana

For much of its early history New Zealand lay mostly under the sea, off the coast of the supercontinent Gondwana, and was, as such, largely denied the spectacular evolution of life on land that occurred elsewhere during this period.

PRECAMBRIAN	CAMBRIAN	ORDOVICIAN	SILURIAN	DEVONIAN	CARBONIFEROUS	PERMIAN	TRIASSIC
570 m.y.a.	500 m.y.a.	430 m.y.a.	390 m.y.a.	345 m.y.a.	300 m.y.a.		

THE story of New Zealand really only begins some 570 million years ago, at the beginning of what is now known as the Cambrian period in geological history. It is from that time that our fossil record begins and although patches of older rocks (ranging up to 680 million years old) are known from the West Coast of the South Island (at Charleston and in the Victoria Range near Reefton), little is known about them as they have been squeezed and distorted by earth movements and heated by intrusions of molten rock so that their records of past life in the form of fossils have been completely wiped out.

In terms of the sheer immensity of geologic time, then, New Zealand is youthful and its record, at least of earlier times, incomplete. By comparison, Australia, its southern neighbour, is much older and dates back almost 3,800 million years to the very beginning of the earth.

In the beginning

As a round figure, a date of 5,000 million years ago is often taken as the birth of the earth. At this time the earth was probably a huge spinning ball of gas and interstellar debris. As time passed, this cosmic mixture gradually condensed into solid matter, and as it compressed heat was generated, so that by 4,000 million years ago temperatures within the nascent earth had risen to the melting point of iron. The earth then probably underwent a profound reorganisation. As the particles of molten iron and other metals sank to the centre, a large part of the earth was converted to a molten state. This was the start of a separation process in which light material floats up to the top (in the case of the earth to form the crust), while heavy material sinks (to form the core). This converted the planet from a roughly homogeneous body, with the same kind of material at all depths, into a zoned or layered body with a series of concentric shells of differing composition and density: the crust, mantle, outer core and inner core.

In time the surface of the primaeval earth cooled sufficiently for rock to solidify, rather like the scum forming on the top of jam during cooking. The oldest rocks in the world — from Australia, Greenland, USA and USSR — were formed at the time, and the newly formed earth must have been very different from the earth we know today, or even that of 1,000 million years ago.

It may have been a much larger planet, not unlike Saturn, with a huge atmosphere of cosmic gas and a rocky central mass which was probably entirely molten. This primordial atmosphere was stripped away, possibly during a period of higher heat output by the sun. Our present atmosphere and surface waters have been derived entirely from the earth itself, that is, from the molten core of the primordial planet. Vast amounts of gas must have been given off from the semi-molten surface of the early earth.

At the same time, as the primitive crust repeatedly cracked and re-melted, a lighter granite liquid would have gradually separated out, floating up to the surface. Further concentration of this granitic material into a thicker granitic (continental) crust may have had to await the commencement of erosion processes, caused by surface water condensed from the exhaled gases. Once under way, the processes of erosion would have provided a means of separating lighter (granitic) from heavier (basaltic) components. Granitic rocks would also have been produced by the re-melting of the sedimentary rocks.

Even after the formation of a totally solid crust and the slow build-up of the first true oceans, intense volcanic activity went on, adding vast amounts of gases and water vapour to the atmosphere. These volcanic gases had a very low oxygen content and for this reason it is thought that the primordial atmosphere was very poor in oxygen. Oxygen was not added to the atmosphere in any volume until advanced forms of oxygen-producing plant life evolved, about 1,900 million years ago.

As metallic particles within the earth sank, large systems of convection currents were set up in the overlying material with cooling material sinking towards the core, to be re-melted, reheated, and rise again to the surface. Again, like scum on the top of jam, thin basalt crust began to form over up-welling currents, where cooling was occurring.

In time, where convection currents converged and after losing their heat descended, the thin rafts of basalt crust were dragged down and re-melted, resulting in a mixing of materials and the generation of intermediate (i.e. halfway between the two extremes of granite and basalt) rock. In this way volcanic chains of andesite rock were formed over the sites of descending currents. Eventually, andesite protocontinents were built up, but because they were located over the sites of down-going currents, their position on the earth's surface would have changed as the convection current pattern also changed.

In the earliest history of the earth convection cells were less stable and more vigorous than they are today and the continents could have 'skidded' all over the surface, like slag on top of molten iron in a blast furnace. As in the blast furnace, the drifting masses of continental 'slag' would sooner or later collide and form even larger masses. Such collisions may have been random but it is possible that the spinning forces generated by the earth's rotation could have deflected these rafts of continental 'slag' towards either pole.

With the world's continents so grouped at either pole, they would have acted like blankets, smothering and trapping heat generated deep within the earth. Like a giant pressure-cooker, the enormous pressure could not be contained. Convection currents welled up, splitting and tearing the continental plates apart, leaving widening rift zones. And in these zones new basaltic oceanic sea-floor crust was formed. As the rifts widened, the leading edges of the continental fragments would have collided with plates on opposing convection currents. In the resulting collision, subduction zones were formed. And as the sea-floor sediments and continental crust were dragged down, melted and mixed together, rocks of true granitic composition were formed for the first time. Thus plate tectonics as we understand it came into play, and with the passage of time, the initial andesite continents gradually became more granitic until they became almost totally so, as they are today.

Once the continental masses became established, they were moved around at the whim of changing patterns of convection currents. In both hemispheres continental fragments collided with neighbouring fragments — at times becoming welded into one mass, at other times breaking up into individual pieces. Today, we can still see the tell-tale signs of where, for example, some 300 million years ago, eastern Siberia was welded on to the remainder of Russia, the welded seam being the Ural mountain belt of today.

Up to now we have assumed that the earth has remained the same size throughout its long history. However, there are some scientists who believe that, quite apart from expansion of the core, there has been slow and steady expansion of the entire globe.

If you take the present shapes of the continents and squeeze them all together, they could all fit together snugly on a globe one half its present size. If this is done, the present continental crust covers the entire surface of the earth, except for some narrow seaways. The fact that the continents do fit together on a smaller globe does seem to be more than a coincidence — and some geologists view this as a major piece of evidence for earth expansion.

Initially, when primaeval crust covered most of the earth and the core was just starting to form, it is possible that the interior of the earth was stirred by one large convection cell. Then, as the core and the entire earth gradually expanded, changes in the convection patterns followed, leading to creation of several smaller cells. As the earth continued to expand, more and more cells were generated so that by 400–300 million years ago a four-cell convection pattern may have been evident. The most recent shift, from four to five cells, possibly occurred 200–100 million years ago and may have been the event that triggered the present episode of continental drift.

If changes in the size of both the globe and the core did, in fact, force changes in the deep circulation patterns of the earth in the way suggested, then it probably follows that over time the zones of convergence and divergence have migrated. Sometimes a certain part of the globe

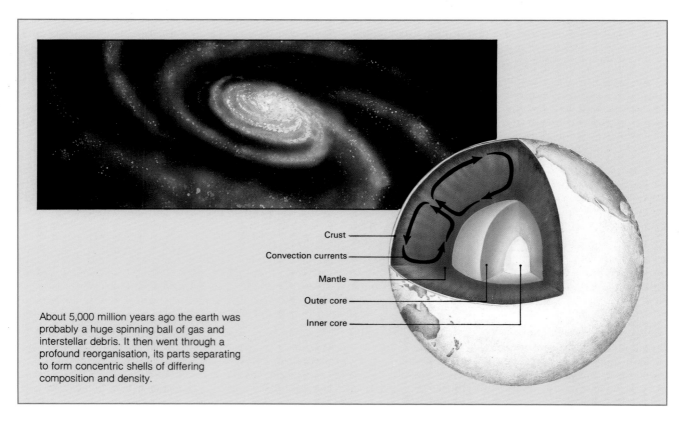

Crust

Convection currents

Mantle

Outer core

Inner core

About 5,000 million years ago the earth was probably a huge spinning ball of gas and interstellar debris. It then went through a profound reorganisation, its parts separating to form concentric shells of differing composition and density.

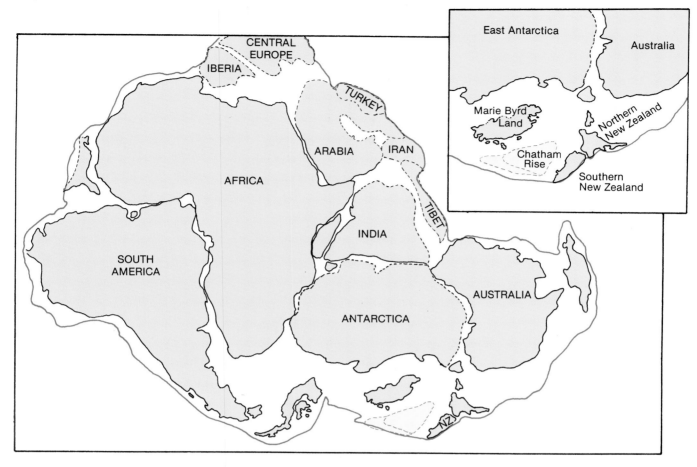

A reconstruction of Gondwana as it appeared before breaking up 180 million years ago. INSET: *New Zealand's position off the coast of Eastern Gondwana.*

would be the site of converging convection currents; crustal material would then be moved towards this area and the resulting collisions would weld individual pieces together. The current system might then change, the site of convergence migrate elsewhere, and in its place arise a zone of current divergence. Crustal material would then be torn apart and drifted for long distances.

Gondwana

Judging from the records of the past preserved in the rocks, we know that from Cambrian times up to about 80 million years ago, New Zealand was positioned between Australia and Antarctica on the eastern edge of the vast super-continent Gondwana. (Its name is derived from that of the *Gonds*, an ancient Dravidian people who established a kingdom in central peninsular India, and *Wana* meaning land.)

Obviously the geography of the world was vastly different from that of today. All of the lands now lying in the Southern Hemisphere, together with India, were grouped into a single landmass, Gondwana. An ancestral ocean, called the Tethys, separated Gondwana from another super-continent called Laurasia, at that time comprising a number of fragmented and separate Northern Hemisphere lands that were later to weld

together. For example, Asiatic USSR, South-East Asia, China, Mongolia and Manchuria — later to become components of Eurasia — were separate landmasses and during much of the Palaeozoic lay much closer to Australasia than they do today. Throughout Cambrian times virtually all of Gondwana was situated in the middle and low latitudes of the Northern Hemisphere, whereas large areas of Europe and Eurasia were situated in the Southern Hemisphere — almost the exact opposite of the modern situation!

Throughout this time, shallow seas covered many areas of what is now Australia and Antarctica and, as far as we know, most of New Zealand was also under the sea, although at times the seas covering New Zealand were dotted with volcanic islands, and submarine lava flows, silts and limestones were laid down on the sea beds around these islands as a result of volcanic activity and erosion. We simply do not have the evidence to determine the size and distribution of these islands, which were themselves constantly rising and subsiding, but if we were to seek a modern equivalent then it would probably be White Island in the Bay of Plenty — with the important distinction that they would have been devoid of land life-forms of any kind.

The beginning of life

What life, then, existed in this vast expanse of sea dotted intermittently with strings of volcanic islands? Certainly no life of any kind existed on land during Cambrian times, nor would it for another 100 million years. Our

17

search for life begins instead in the shallow seas fringing the landmasses then present.

During the early Precambrian Era complex organic compounds, notably amino acids — the building-blocks of plants and animals — had been developed from simple inorganic substances. Simple organisms such as algae and bacteria appeared later, between 3,500–2,500 million years ago, and by 650 million years ago soft-bodied marine and freshwater animals such as worms, jellyfish and sponges had evolved.

Then, at the beginning of the Cambrian, 570 million years ago, an important evolutionary development occurred. Hard parts (skeletons, shelly coverings, etc.) first appeared in abundance at this time and over the next 30 million years most of the organisms preserved as fossils developed hard parts, primarily composed of calcium/magnesium carbonate or phosphate. Some paleontologists view this development as simply a step in the evolution of life, needing no special explanation. Others, impressed by the sudden development of such a diverse range of organisms, feel that some chemical and environmental factors acted as trigger mechanisms. One of these chemical factors may have been the levels of oxygen in the atmosphere. The various chemicals that together build hard parts in marine creatures are extracted from the sea. This requires specific chemical and physical conditions in both the sea and atmosphere, and the level

of oxygen is one such condition. One idea that has been proposed is that the original atmosphere of the earth lacked oxygen, and that the build-up to the present level of 21 per cent is entirely due to the activities of plants, notably marine algae. If this idea is close to what actually happened then it is thought that by the beginning of the Cambrian oxygen levels had reached such a point that animals could manufacture collagen, an essential component of both hard parts and large muscles.

What new organisms flourished in the new ecological niches that the build-up of oxygen provided? For the most part, the animals living on the sea floor were small and often only a few millimetres in length. The shallow sea-beds of the continental shelves surrounding most of the continents and islands then in existence provided good conditions for plant growth and many algae flourished in the shallow sunlit waters. It was here, then, that the animals of the Cambrian seas foraged for food in the sea-floor muds. Dominant among them were the brachiopods, sponges and arthropods. The arthropods (jointed-legged creatures), which include the modern crayfish, insects, millipedes and centipedes, were represented in Cambrian times by the aquatic trilobites, so-named because their bodies were divided into three lobes. These distinctive creatures superficially resembled modern wood-lice, and dominated the seas for the next 100 million years, becoming extinct 235 million years ago.

Ancestors of spiny-skinned creatures (Echinoderms) also evolved at this time and were later to give rise to sea urchins and sea eggs, starfish, sea lilies and sea cucumbers. Also appearing in the Cambrian period were the first molluscs — a group that later expanded to include chitons, tusk shells, clams, mussels, scallops, whelks, snails, slugs, limpets, squids, cuttlefish and ammonites.

Although only a small slice of the total amount of Cambrian time is preserved in New Zealand, we do, nonetheless, have a good cross-section of the animals living at the time. These fossils are found mainly in limey muds that were originally laid down in the shallow seas surrounding the volcanic islands and archipelagoes off-shore from the coastline of eastern Australia and Antarctica.

Cambrian fossils are known from Springs Junction (west Nelson) and Cobb Valley (north-west Nelson). The Cambrian rocks of the Cobb Valley are perhaps the most famous, as near the head of Cobb Reservoir stands a large limestone block — called appropriately 'Trilobite Rock' — crammed with the remains of trilobites. As well as trilobites, the rocks also contain sponges, brachiopods, molluscs and conodonts — all of which lived on the sea floor, foraging for organic detritus or sifting out fine food materials.

(Continued on page 23.)

For much of geologic history New Zealand was a slab of sea-floor off the coast of Eastern Gondwana, although at times the seas covering New Zealand were dotted with volcanic islands, probably similar in size to present-day White Island in the Bay of Plenty (inset).

PALAEOZOIC MARINE LIFE

A very real difficulty in trying to portray what marine life looked like in New Zealand waters during the Palaeozoic Era is that our own fossil record from these times is largely incomplete. With only a small slice of the Palaeozoic preserved in our rocks, we are forced to look to other parts of Gondwana to see what may have then lived in our waters.

New Zealand's oldest macrofossils, those that can be seen with the naked eye, as opposed to microfossils, are found in the Cambrian 'Trilobite Rock' of the Cobb Valley, Nelson. These fossils include trilobites, brachiopods, clams and snails, and all were small bottom-dwelling shallow-water creatures. In their adult condition they neither swam nor crawled very far, nor were carried around by ocean currents. In their larval stage, however, brachiopods and molluscs, and probably the extinct trilobites, could have moved quite long distances in the plankton of the surface waters of the oceans until they came to an area suitable for settlement and growth. Migration was generally a passive affair depending on the length of larval life and the speed and direction of ocean currents.

Barriers to their migration would have been, as now, currents travelling in the wrong direction, temperature or other climatic conditions which they could not tolerate and, of course, landmasses in the way.

So where did they come from? During Cambrian times the New Zealand region was part of the continental sea floor off East Gondwana and not surprisingly our trilobites and brachiopods show a very clear East Australian-East Asia relationship. Favourable ocean conditions and land-sea relations enabled these shallow-water organisms to have easy contact between these three areas, which were much closer together then. This same Australia-China affinity continues through the Palaeozoic among these shelly fossils, but the Chinese relationship gets weaker. Some barrier to migration between New Zealand and China must have been developing, and we believe that barrier to have been a widening and deepening sea as moving plates carried the two regions further apart.

Ordovician graptolite (Aorangi Mine, Nelson).

The great explosion of life forms in the Cambrian gave rise to many short-lived groups, but those which survived the Cambrian have generally continued through to the present day (major exceptions are the trilobites and graptolites).

Invertebrate groups which had not already appeared in the Cambrian quickly appeared later. Corals, for instance, are possibly present in the Australian Cambrian but become more numerous in the Ordovician 460 million years ago and remain prominent from there on. Initially there were solitary corals only; they become colonial and formed reefs in warmer shallower waters from late Silurian (420 million years) onwards.

Corals grow a little each day, and growth varies slightly according to both the monthly lunar cycle and the annual seasonal cycle. Thus we see a sequence of very fine ridges, each 28–30 of which are grouped into bands (monthly) and these bands show a regular broadening and narrowing each dozen bands (annual). But when, for example, Devonian corals are counted we find that each of the coarsest (annual) bands covers 13 groupings of about 400 fine ridges. Astrophysics tells us that the earth's rate of spin has slowed over geological time by two seconds per day each 100,000 years, so that there would have been 424 days in the year at the beginning of the Cambrian, 385 days/year at the end of the Palaeozoic, and 400 days/year in the early Devonian! So here we have the physicists calculations confirmed by fossils!

We tend to think of vertebrates as the most advanced animals, yet they too had appeared by the end of the Silurian, 430 million years ago. Then in Devonian lakes and rivers a great evolutionary radiation occurred and these early fishes established themselves as the dominant aquatic animals throughout the world's marine and fresh waters. The most primitive forms, the armoured ostracoderms, had a backbone of cartilage but no jaws — they are represented today by the lampreys — but cartilaginous jaws very quickly developed and Devonian fish belong to five different classes, including

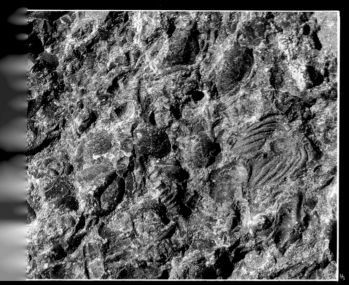

ABOVE: *'Trilobite Rock', Cobb Valley, north-west Nelson.*
RIGHT: *A Devonian trilobite (Reefton). So-named because their bodies were divided into three parts, trilobites dominated the seas for 100 million years.*

he earliest sharks and bony fishes, the lungfish of Australian and African rivers, and the first coelacanths (with living members in deep Indian Ocean waters). Lamprey, lungfish, coelacanth and sturgeon are all 'living fossils', small remnants of once much more diverse fish groups which have largely failed in competition with advanced bony fishes.

These early forms were nearly all quite heavily armour-plated over the head and shoulder and with much larger, thicker body scales than a modern fish. The lawless ostracoderms were generally bottom-dwelling types with no or only small paired fins. The placoderms, from which sharks and rays developed, were more varied; some looked like ostracoderms but with bigger jointed paddle-like fins (the antiarchs); others developed a movable joint between head and neck (the arthrodires), entered the sea and became giant predators up to 10 metres long. The earliest sharks of the Devonian were also marine types, as today, whereas all the bony fishes of that time (coelacanths, lungfish, forerunners to the sturgeon and the little acanthodians, with spines in place of paired fins) were fresh-water dwellers.

These early fish groups are found all over the world, and this suggests that both land and sea environments and therefore climates were much more uniform in pre-Permian times than they are now. On the other hand, vertebrates can move around more actively over greater distances than most invertebrates. They can migrate as adults as well as in the juvenile stage, and we can then expect them to have migrated faster and further. However, early marine vertebrates would have been just as closely tied to shallower waters as were the early invertebrates because of both the lack of oxygen in the deep bottom waters and the higher pressures against which they had not yet developed any protection.

The Devonian limestones and mudstone near Reefton have recently been shown to contain arthrodire acanthodian and primitive bony fish scales and plates all closely similar to Australian Devonian forms. These are the only vertebrate remains so far known from the New Zealand Palaeozoic, but they show that this area did share with the rest of the world in their distribution.

The ostracoderms, placoderms and acanthodians mostly died out at the end of the Devonian, 345 million years ago, and were replaced by more advanced forms. This early diversity and explosive radiation followed by rapid extinction of some groups has a close parallel with the early development of the invertebrates during the Cambrian. The exploitation of a new feature — shells in invertebrates, backbone and jaws in vertebrates — allows the rapid development of a variety of new forms, some of which are quickly found to be less effective and become extinct.

Out of this diversity two groups proved to be the 'fittest': the sharks, rays and their relatives; and the modern bony fishes or teleosts (salmon, snapper, eel etc.). Two other groups, the lungfish in fresh water and the coelacanths in marine and fresh waters, were abundant during the Palaeozoic but have dwindled over the last 200 million years to near-extinction.

Among the major fish groups the sharks were the last to appear, only evolving in the late Devonian. The

During Cambrian times creatures had developed 'hard parts', and these included ancestors of the modern molluscs and echinoderms. ABOVE: *A bed of common blue mussels.* ABOVE LEFT: *A snakeskin chiton.* LEFT: *A biscuit star.*

reached a maximum in the Carboniferous and have maintained that diversity ever since, increasing only by the appearance of the rays in the Jurassic.

Another fish group to appear late in the Devonian is the rhipidistians, a group with fleshy lobes at the base of the fins and related to coelacanths. The fleshy base surrounds three bones from which the fin radiates. Amphibians (frogs, etc.) have evolved directly from the rhipidistians and these three bones became the major bones of their and *our* limbs. Thus the rhipidistians hold a truly intermediate position between fully aquatic fish and the amphibians. They are classed as fish because they had fins, but their soft parts seem to have been essentially amphibian and the step from the rhipidistian fin to the amphibian limb is relatively small. This group lasted into the Carboniferous and seems to have died out in competition with the early amphibians, which lived rather similar lives.

The earliest amphibian, *Ichthyostega*, is known from the very end of the Devonian. Although it had legs rather than fins its fish ancestry is clear — it still had a fin along the top of the tail and the spinal column remained weak. But with the beginning of exploitation of the new land habitat amphibians produced yet another rapid diversification in the Carboniferous and Permian.

These amphibians had lost the fin, strengthened the backbone for body support on land, and evolved much more efficient lungs and breathing than in lungfish and rhipidistians. They remained tied to the water for egg and larval development (tadpole stage). They reached two to three metres in length, and were successful pre-

dators for their day, but in competition with the developing reptiles they failed and are hardly known after the Permian.

From these amphibians evolved the first reptiles. The amniote egg of reptiles and birds is internally fertilised, has a larger yolk sac so that the young remains protected for a longer period and avoids the free-living tadpole stage, and has a shell tough enough to protect the contents.

The transformation of gill structures into jaws raised early vertebrates from small bottom-dwellers to active wide-ranging fish. The transformation of gills to lungs and fins to legs saw the vertebrates move from water to land. The development of the amniote egg liberated land vertebrates from dependence on water for their life cycle and enabled them to wander freely over the land.

Thus we reach the end of the Permian where a catastrophic extinction occurred. More than half of the late Permian families fail to cross over into the Triassic. Why this happened is not clear, but it was one of a number of such events in the history of life. Other drastic changes included most importantly the acquisition of a skeleton at the beginning of the Cambrian and the subsequent diversification of invertebrates, the Devonian radiation of fish groups, and the Carboniferous-Permian evolution of land vertebrates. New Zealand shared in most of these. Climatic change and changes in land-sea relations were among the causes, but important also were the impacts that changes in one group of organisms had on those other groups around them — the domino effect.

Some rocks, especially black shales and slates, also preserve remains of the ancient plankton. These animals called graptolites, lived suspended in a position close to or at the surface of the sea. They were a group of individual polyps, each one connected with others of the colony by a stalk. Each polyp had a pad of tentacle-like branches by means of which it breathed and which it used for feeding by gathering minute food particles from the ocean. After death, the graptolite colonies sank to the sea floor and were squashed flat into the sea floor muds, so that today they can be seen only as white or grey films on the split surfaces of rock, at first sight looking like fine pencil markings on the rock faces.

Most of us would not associate graptolites with gold deposits, but the first graptolites discovered in New Zealand were found in 1874 during the earliest gold mining activity at Golden Ridge in north-west Nelson.

The Southern Hemisphere

From the Cambrian to the Permian Eras, a period of more than 300 million years, the vast super-continents of Gondwana and Laurasia were partners in a global elephantine waltz that was to see their respective geographic positions reversed as they sedately gyrated around the globe. Today we can only wonder as to why this happened, although some scientists maintain that the dramatic rotations of the continents then resulted from the development from a three- to a four-cell convection pattern in the earth's mantle. Nevertheless, whatever the reason, whereas in Cambrian times New Zealand and much of Gondwana had been positioned in the mid latitudes of the Northern Hemisphere, by Silurian times (420 million years ago) Gondwana had rotated so dramatically that New Zealand now lay at a latitude

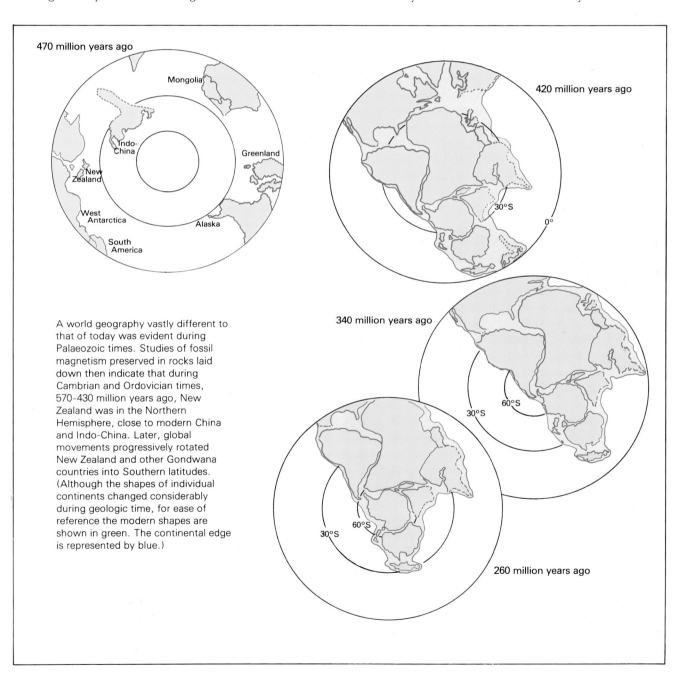

A world geography vastly different to that of today was evident during Palaeozoic times. Studies of fossil magnetism preserved in rocks laid down then indicate that during Cambrian and Ordovician times, 570-430 million years ago, New Zealand was in the Northern Hemisphere, close to modern China and Indo-China. Later, global movements progressively rotated New Zealand and other Gondwana countries into Southern latitudes. (Although the shapes of individual continents changed considerably during geologic time, for ease of reference the modern shapes are shown in green. The continental edge is represented by blue.)

of modern-day Central Asia. China, Manchuria, Mongolia and South-East Asia had also moved northwards away from Australasia. And as Gondwana moved south, parts of it now began to lie over the South Pole. By Carboniferous times, 350–300 million years ago, a large bulk of Gondwana virtually straddled the polar region and New Zealand was sited at a chilly latitude of 50° South.

The more Gondwana drifted south the more its climate changed so that whereas in Cambrian and Ordovician times New Zealand had basked in warm-temperate to subtropical climates, by Silurian times cool-temperate climatic conditions prevailed. At the same time earth movements were reshaping much of eastern Gondwana, creating substantial areas of mountainous land, particularly in the southern regions. The presence of this high country so close to the South Pole generated unstable stormy weather conditions, favouring the formation of large quantities of snow and ice. The valleys and gullies of the high country provided concentrating grounds where the snow and ice were compacted to form hard glacier ice. Once formed, the glacier ice would have slowly flowed outwards, covering the surrounding lands and pushing out across the sea as floating ice sheets. Eventually, this polar ice cap was so huge that it was able to reflect vast amounts of the sun's energy out into space, where it was permanently lost to the earth. The earth chilled and a protracted series of ice ages ensued.

For the next 100 million years until the end of the Permian Era, 235 million years ago, Gondwana was gripped by a remorseless ice age that endured far longer than any the world has since witnessed. The desolation was almost complete and the forces reshaping the land truly monumental as glaciers scoured out vast terrains of rock in their slow gargantuan passage to the sea. Today, such glacial deposits of till and moraine, dating from this time, typify many regions in India, South Africa, South America, Australia and Antarctica.

By middle Permian times New Zealand lay deep in the polar region, its position having changed to 60–70° latitude south — the furthest south it was to get for another 150 million years. However, as before, most of New Zealand, with the exception of a few strings of volcanic islands, was under the sea.

With little land poking up out of the sea New Zealand now became the dumping ground for much of the material being eroded off the Australian and Antarctic landmasses. The waters of the ocean covering the site of New Zealand were probably at times full of icebergs, breaking off and floating away from the edges of the ice sheets then covering large areas of Australia, Tasmania and Antarctica. Modern icebergs carry away from their parent ice sheets or glaciers vast quantities of rock debris, derived from mountain landslides or from the scraping and scouring of the bedrock. As the iceberg melts and shrinks in volume, this debris drops to the sea bed and is incorporated into the muds and sands of the sea floor. Such an origin has been proposed for some of the rocks that were laid down on the sea bed covering Southland during Permian times. These rocks contain large blocks of apparently 'exotic' types of rocks, which appear to have been dropped into the muds mantling the sea bed.

The earliest plants had simple leafless stems and water was conducted within them by crude tubes. The descendants of these first plants include Lycopodium, *or clubmoss (left) and horsetail (below).*

Life on land

New Zealand was largely submerged when terrestrial plant life first appeared during late Silurian times, 410–400 million years ago. An absence of marine fossils in our record during most of Devonian and Carboniferous times suggests that during some of that time at least major earth movements in the New Zealand region — the Tuhua Orogeny — had created areas of broken rugged landscape. Whether life evolved on this new land we don't know and anyway by Permian times the land had eroded away. Indeed, terrestrial plant life would not be represented in any quantity in our fossil record for another 175 million years and the only terrestrial fossils we have dated before then are a few scraps of *Glossopteris* leaf fragments from Permian times, found in marine rocks in eastern Southland. The leaves had probably drifted offshore from the main landmass of Gondwana and on becoming waterlogged had settled on the sea floor, there to be incorporated in sands and mud.

About 400 million years ago, in late Silurian times, the first rudimentary plants began to colonise the land. Prior to that, plant life had been confined to the sea, with algae appearing about 2,000 million years ago and plants ancestral to the modern fungi, mosses and liverworts in late Precambrian times, 1,000–600 million years ago. The first colonists of the land were probably modified seaweeds, living in tidal marshlands, where in between tides the plants had to anchor themselves, to stand reasonably erect and to survive in the air. Eventually they were able to advance to higher and drier land, sending up aerial shoots to scatter their spores and thrusting root systems down into the earth to seek out water.

Apart from breathing air, the main problem confronting the early plants was reproduction in the absence of water. As it was, they probably had a reproductive system similar to that of modern ferns — that is, their spores grew into tiny heart-shaped sheets called gametophytes, which clung to the damp earth. In turn, the gametophytes produced spore bearers by manufacturing sperm and egg cells which could only unite in water. This dependence on water may have restricted the plants to moist lowlands until the evolution of true seeds, using air-borne pollen to fertilise the egg cells. These first plants had simple leafless stems and water was conducted within them by means of crude tubes. As plants took to drier ground, simple leaves developed to catch the sunlight, roots developed and internal tubes became specialised to circulate sap.

The first authentic land plants form a complex called the psilophytes. Some were rudimentary and without leaves or roots. Others grew up to 2–3 metres in height and resembled small trees with swollen stems. Although many of the early plants were small and spindly and had exotic shapes compared with modern plants, they were nonetheless recognisable as plants. As many of them were what people would call fern-like, the Devonian is often called 'The Age of Ferns'.

Away from the cold climates, in the more equable climate of Laurasia, plant life developed a rich assemblage of giant tree-ferns, horsetails, clubmosses, lycopods, seed ferns and cone-bearing plants that grew luxuriantly in

BELOW: *A detail from a forest-floor assemblage showing moss, liverwort and* Asplenium *fern nestling amid old tree fern fronds.* RIGHT: *The simple fronds of the kidney fern catch sunlight and rainwater.* BELOW RIGHT: *A fern assemblage on the forest floor.*

the tropical and subtropical belts of the world. The forests produced quantities of woody plant debris which accumulated in swamps as thick layers of peat. When the peat was buried beneath later sediments it was slowly transformed into coal, and in this way the coal deposits of North America and Europe, Asia and Australia were formed. It is for this reason the period of geological history is termed the Carboniferous.

During the Carboniferous and Permian periods insects evolved, including dragonflies, butterflies and moths which proliferated and rapidly expanded into the ecological niches created by the forests. Amphibians also became a large and important group and towards the end of the Carboniferous gave rise to the reptiles. By later Permian times large squat reptiles, heavily armoured and some attaining a height of 1.5 metres, were lumbering over many lands, especially those in the tropical and subtropical zones of Laurasia (including southern European USSR, southern Europe, Texas, Oklahoma and New Mexico).

The grip of glacial winter naturally precluded the new reptiles from colonising Gondwana and it was only in Triassic times that they ventured south when the glaciers had retreated. Yet even in the desolation of the glacial period plant life thrived. Continuous ice sheets did not cover the entire landscape and in the ice-free areas adjacent to the ice sheets hardy plants thrived. These plants, called *Glossopteris*, had thick, fleshy, fibrous,

tongue-shaped leaves which have been preserved in great quantities, forming in some instances thick layered beds. The discovery of these fossil beds so close to glacial deposits suggests that it was a plant which, although obviously plentiful, only grew adjacent to the Gondwana ice sheets, as it is not known from other areas. It was probably like the hardy sedges, rushes, mountain daisies and snow grass that grow in profusion close to our modern glaciers in little ice-free hollows and on bare slopes adjacent to the tongues of ice.

Glossopteris fossils were first found in India and Australia, and discoveries followed in South Africa, South America and Tasmania. However, the hardest-won specimens were undoubtedly those obtained in 1912 by Scott's ill-fated expedition to the South Pole. They were collected by Dr Edward Wilson, scientist and artist, from the cliffs of a massive sandstone formation flanking the Beardmore Glacier. The specimens, along with others, totalling 16 kilograms in weight, were collected during the harrowing return journey from the South Pole. They were carried on the expedition's sledge right to the end, until Scott and his companions could walk no more. The next summer the bodies were found in their tent, the fossils on the sledge nearby.

The discovery of *Glossopteris* on the different continents has been used by scientists, including Wegener and du Toit, as evidence of continental drift and of the original composition of Gondwana. Interestingly, the discovery of a few *Glossopteris* leaf fragments in Southland (see page 25) has proved conclusively that New Zealand too had originally been part of Gondwana, although as we now know, apart from a few largely ephemeral volcanic islands, it was mainly part of the sea floor off Australia and Antarctica.

LEFT: *A reconstruction of* Glossopteris *that grew adjacent to the Gondwana ice sheets in the same way that our modern alpine flora grows close to glaciers.* BELOW: Glossopteris *leaves preserved in Permian rock, Mercer Ridge, Ohio Range, Antarctica.*

2. The ancestral continent

About 140 million years ago a huge new landmass was rucked up in the New Zealand region and from Gondwana waves of plant and animal species migrated, colonising the new environment. The moa, kiwi and tuatara had arrived.

| PERMIAN | TRIASSIC | JURASSIC | CRETACEOUS |

235 m.y.a.   190 m.y.a.   135 m.y.a.

FOR most of the Carboniferous and Permian New Zealand had been in the grip of a terrible ice age that at times shrouded large areas of Gondwana in a mantle of ice and snow. But from the beginning of the Mesozoic Era, 235 million years ago, these ice sheets began to retreat as the super-continent gradually first skewed on its axis, like some ungainly dancer, and then gradually shunted away northwards, turning its back on the South Pole. Just as in Carboniferous times, when the presence of high country in the polar regions had been critical to the accumulation of ice, so now these same ice sheets began to melt as the high country moved away from the polar regions. As more and more of Gondwana shifted northwards, so its overall climate improved. It was a slow process and conditions didn't change dramatically, but by Jurassic times, 192–135 million years ago, the climate of Gondwana had improved so much that temperate conditions extended well into latitudes which are now the preserve of polar climates. At the same time there was a corresponding expansion of the tropical and subtropical zones, with warm conditions extending north and south into latitudes that today have temperate climates.

Probably because all the water that had formerly been locked up in glaciers and ice sheets had flowed back into the oceans, world sea levels peaked in the Jurassic, when almost 25 per cent of the present continental areas were covered by sea. Most of what is now western Europe was covered by shallow seas which also traversed the margins of Africa, Asia, India, Australia, North and South America.

Most of these seas were interconnected at various times and collectively are called 'Tethyan'. The animals living in these Tethyan seas also extended to New Zealand, but not until middle and late Jurassic times.

The 'Age of Reptiles'

These warmer climates spurred reptilian evolution and for this reason the Mesozoic Era is often called 'the Age of Reptiles'. As the ice sheets disappeared, numerous reptilian groups appeared in both Laurasia and Gondwana and once established as viable and efficient land dwellers reigned unchallenged for almost 200 million years. Today, despite the wide diversity of existing species, there are nevertheless certain characteristics common to practically all reptiles. They are cold-blooded vertebrates, which means that the body temperature is limited to a great extent by the temperature of their surroundings. Because body processes slow down as temperature falls, during cool or cold weather they remain more or less dormant. But with a rise in temperature the various bodily organs and activities are quickened. Through a process called 'thermo-regulation' they can also utilise direct heat from the sun or reflected off rocks to raise their body temperature several degrees above the surrounding air temperature, and common to many species is the ability to widen and flatten the ribcage in order to maximise the amount of body contact with any heat source such as rocks.

An important step towards living on land was the development of reptilian skin. Contrary to popular opinion their skin is not 'slimy' but dry, lacking skin glands, and covered by protective horny scales and plates which greatly reduce evaporation through the skin. Similarly, the eggs, laid on the land, are protected from drying out by a leathery or limy shell.

At first, in the early Triassic, 235–215 million years ago, comparatively few reptiles were able to migrate between the two super-continents and Laurasia and Gondwana had distinct reptilian populations. Laurasia's reptiles, for example, gave rise to the dinosaurs, while Gondwana's reptiles were mammal-like in appearance, with skulls and bodies similar to those of wolves or foxes. One of the most spectacular Gondwana reptiles was the wolf-like *Cynognathus*, whose fossils are only found in Argentina and South Africa. This reptile had a skull similar to that of a dog (hence the name, *cyno* = dog, *gnathus* = jaws) and its teeth were adapted to a carnivorous diet. The body was slender and supple, and the feet suited for rapid running.

Another reptile that occurs with *Cynognathus* in South Africa is *Lystrosaurus*, which was a heavily built animal, about the size of a large sheep with a barrel-like body, stout stocky legs, broad feet and a short tail. The head is very distinctive, with beak-like jaws and a pair of large tusks. *Lystrosaurus* has long been known from South Africa, India and Western China, where it is an important Triassic fossil. Its discovery in Antarctica in 1970 provided a major palaeontological link, binding together the Triassic Gondwana.

Before the finding of *Lystrosaurus* in Antarctica, its presence in the other countries could be readily explained in terms of the modern world map. The reptile could

27

simply walk up through the African continent, across Asia Minor and into India and Western China. Such a wide geographic distribution would not be at all unusual as the leopard, for example, not so long ago ranged from the Cape of Good Hope, through Africa, across the Middle East and Asia and well into Siberia. *Lystrosaurus*, however, could not have walked into Antarctica without some help from continental drift. Although it was a lover of lakes and rivers and may have been like a miniature hippopotamus, it was essentially a land animal and with its heavy body would have sunk like a stone in deep water. It could no more cross great stretches of ocean than a hippopotamus today. It had to move from one region to another by a land route, albeit one that was well watered, and this it could only have done if at some point the continents had been joined together.

Although dinosaurs had initially evolved in Laurasia, by late Triassic times (200 million years ago), the lines between Gondwana and Laurasia had become so blurred that many land reptiles were probably able to roam far and wide across both super-continents.

The dinosaurs as a group are thought to have been derived from late Permian and Triassic reptiles called Thecodontia. Although these reptiles were about the size and shape of a crocodile, unlike today's crocodiles they were primarily land dwellers and probably extremely active predators. In the late Triassic the Thecodontia gave rise to five groups. The first group developed eventually into the birds. The second group is the crocodiles that have survived with very little change right through to the present day, except that in the Mesozoic many of them were thoroughly sea-going.

The third group was the flying reptiles or pterosaurs, climaxing in the late Cretaceous with some forms having wing spans of 15 metres. The fourth and fifth groups comprise the dinosaurs or 'terrible lizards' (Greek *deinos sauros*). These two groups are called Saurischia ('reptile hips') and Ornithischia ('bird hips'). Together they ruled the earth throughout the Jurassic and Cretaceous periods and in the equable conditions then existing some grew to enormous size and became rapacious predators, while others became vegetarians.

The Saurischia, or reptile-hipped dinosaurs, gave rise to the theropods, consisting entirely of two-legged carnivores. Although some theropods were fairly small and lightly built, rather like an ostrich, they also included some of the largest and most fearsome land-living carnivores of all time — notably *Tyrannosaurus rex*, standing about six metres tall and weighing about seven tonnes.

Also included in the Saurischia are the sauropods — entirely four-legged and solely herbivorous. Some of these grew to be the largest land animals of all time — *Brontosaurus, Diplodocus* and the 80-tonne *Brachiosaurus*.

The Ornithischia or bird-hipped dinosaurs were all herbivorous and included both four- and two-legged

Stegosaurus *roamed over Laurasia during Mesozoic times. Debate continues as to whether the vertical plates along the back were for defence or were a mechanism for regulating temperature.*

RECONSTRUCTION BY GEOFFREY COX

types. They were the most abundant of all the dinosaurs and included the distinctive duck-billed dinosaurs, whose habitat was semi-aquatic and which probably fed on the reeds and grasses bordering lakes and lagoons. Preyed upon by the rapacious theropods, many Ornithischia developed impressive armatures. Some had rhinoceros-like bony spikes on their heads and great frill-like extensions protecting their necks; others developed a double row of enormous vertical bony plates along the back and long bony spikes on the end of the tail. The most remarkable armoured dinosaurs or 'reptilian tanks' were covered entirely with thick armour-plating, liberally studded with spikes and with a heavy club-like tail, again equipped with spikes, that could be flailed around like a mace.

Throughout the Mesozoic the dinosaurs continued to move further south, successfully colonising large parts of Gondwana so that by Jurassic times (190–135 million years ago) they had reached Australia. Australian discoveries to date include huge lumbering plant-eating sauropods (one from Queensland was 17 metres long, stood three metres high at the hip and weighed 20 tonnes),

two-legged carnivorous theropods, a small armoured dinosaur (ankylosaur) and a two-legged plant-eater (iguanodont), about seven metres in length.

Strangely, our own fossil record from these times is silent. The only evidence we have of dinosaurs are records dating from the Cretaceous, nearly 65 million years later (see pages 48-50). One probable explanation for this absence is that until the Jurassic most of New Zealand lay under the sea — a mere appendage to the Gondwana continental shelf. As well, it had been the last part of Gondwana to move north and for much of Triassic times had languished in cool-temperate climates, the most southerly (70°-80°S latitude) of the Gondwana lands. These cool climates probably proved unattractive to most of the cold-bloodied reptiles that were around at this time, so that even if land had been present in New Zealand and the 'right' dispersal routes had been available, the dinosaurs were unlikely to have migrated here.

The ancestral continent

During Jurassic times New Zealand's long sojourn under the sea was terminated by a series of earth movements that were eventually to create an ancestral New Zealand landmass of truly continental proportions — a Greater New Zealand (see pages 32-33). Earth movements that had been evident during the Triassic rucked up and pushed above sea level much of the sedimentary and volcanic material that had been deposited on the sea floor since Carboniferous and Permian times. More and more land appeared throughout Triassic times, until eventually by the middle and late Jurassic an extensive new landmass had been created. And what a landmass — half the size of modern Australia, it stretched northwards towards New Caledonia, to Lord Howe Rise in the west, to the Chatham Islands in the east, and to the southern edge of the Campbell Plateau in the south. By comparison, modern New Zealand only occupies a mere 10 per cent of the total size of this ancestral land — the remainder having been submerged by the sea to form the largest drowned continent in the world.

Because the Tasman Sea and the Southern Ocean were not then in existence the new land was also in close physical contact with Australia and Antarctica, and other links also existed via long fingers of land and interlinked chains of islands extending northwards from New Caledonia towards New Guinea and Indonesia.

The spectacular emergence of this Greater New Zealand with its extensions to nearby parts of Gondwana now effectively ended New Zealand's long isolation. The new land links provided access for waves of immigrants that fanned out to colonise the wealth of newly created environments. Among the first wave of colonisers would have been plants, many of which, like the reptiles, had evolved elsewhere in both Gondwana and Laurasia in warm Triassic climates. Some of these may indeed have been present in New Zealand in Triassic times when it was only a few offshore islands. A good example is the fern-like plant *Dicroidium*, which is known from Triassic rocks of all Gondwana countries. Many of the early ferns, lycopods, clubmosses and horsetails would also have migrated during this time, taking advantage of the warmer climate. Other Laurasian migrants were conifers. From them, the araucarian pines appeared that gave rise to the modern kauri, the Norfolk pine and the monkey puzzle tree. These were followed by another group of specialised conifers, called podocarps, ancestral to many of the New Zealand forest trees, such as totara, miro, matai, kahikatea, rimu, tanekaha, toatoa etc. The pines, spruces and araucarian pines all bear fully developed cones, but in the podocarps the cones are greatly reduced, often to merely a single scale. The seed, however, is often surrounded by a fleshy cover or is borne on a fleshy stalk, hence the scientific name for the group, *Podocarpus*, which means 'seed with a foot'.

The first New Zealanders

In the succeeding waves of immigrants to colonise the new land would have been the land animals which in Jurassic times were dominated by insects and wideranging groups of amphibians and reptiles. These early

The ancestors of the podocarps and araucarian pines probably migrated to New Zealand in the early Jurassic, 195–172 million years ago. LEFT: *'Tane Mahuta', the largest known kauri, standing at 52 metres and some 1,200 years old.* BELOW: *A tanekaha female cone.* RIGHT: *Kahikatea forest, Westland.*

arrivals have been drastically thinned over the geological ages, but even today we can pinpoint some of their descendants which still populate our forests and islands.

Some of these animals are endemic and now only found in New Zealand, their roots deep in the geological past. These are termed 'living fossils' because they are the only survivors of primitive groups that evolved in late Palaeozoic and early Mesozoic times and subsequently gave rise to, and elsewhere in the world were eventually replaced by, more advanced groups unable to reach New Zealand. These 'archaic' groups include, for example, the native frog (*Leiopelma*) and the tuatara (*Sphenodon*).

Other New Zealand native animals, again of very ancient lineages and with life habits that make them unable to cross any extensive stretch of salt water, belong to groups that are today only found scattered across remnants of the old Gondwana. These creatures, showing 'southern' affinities (i.e. with relatives in southern South America, the sub-Antarctic islands, Australia and South Africa), date back to the time when Gondwana was one continent, and include some birds, the *Peripatus* and some native earthworms, insects, snails and slugs.

A frog without a tadpole

Charles Darwin in his *On the Origin of Species* remarked that frogs are absent from truly oceanic islands — those that have not had any land links in the geological past. This is because they are extremely sensitive to sea water. Unable to 'raft' across the ocean on floating logs, the New Zealand native frogs obviously needed continuous land,

(Continued on page 34.)

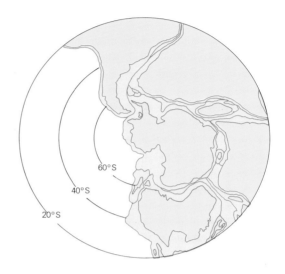

The Southern Hemisphere landmass 180 million years ago during the early Jurassic when plant and animal migrations were possible across the width and breadth of Gondwana.

31

A GREATER NEW ZEALAND

THE continental landmass created during the Mesozoic was not built, as it were, overnight. Instead, our knowledge of historic earthquakes suggests that it was accomplished by a series of small upward movements, of perhaps 3–5 metres at a time, accompanied by massive jolting earthquakes spaced out at intervals of 100 or more years. These small movements, extending over millions of years, gradually raised the piles of sedimentary material, poking them up out of the sea until by late Jurassic times a Greater New Zealand landmass was formed — a land about one half the size of Australia. Where did this land come from?

Beginning some time in the Carboniferous, the eastern edge of Gondwana — began to over-ride the sea floor of the ancestral Pacific Ocean in the same way that the leading edge of an ice floe over-rides a neighbouring floe. A collision boundary or subduction zone developed between the edge of Gondwana and the Pacific Oceanic Plate, and along this boundary the sea floor buckled downwards, creating a deep submarine trench. The hard foundation rocks forming the continental edge of Gondwana, like a giant bulldozer blade, scraped off great thicknesses of sands and muds from the upper surface of the descending sea floor. These distorted sediments were thrust up, buckled and crunched along the continental edge, forming a zone of broken and eroded terrain. At the same time, as the sea floor descended deeper into the earth's mantle, it encountered progressively hotter temperatures until it melted. The resulting molten rock or 'magma' rose to the surface — as bubbles do when water boils — and at the surface would have formed strings of actively erupting volcanoes, on both land and on the sea floor. These were the islands found in New Zealand waters during Carboniferous, Permian and Triassic times — archipelagoes of intermittently erupting volcanoes.

As well as the debris being spewed from these volcanoes vast amounts of sediment were being eroded from Gondwana — some from high country in eastern Australia and Tasmania, but most came from West Antarctica, mainly from land that was then actively rising in the regions of Marie Byrd Land and Ellsworth Land. All this material was carried off into the sea and was dumped in vast quantities on the sea floor in the areas now occupied by New Zealand and New Caledonia.

As we know, Gondwana was, during Permian times, caught in the onslaught of a series of ice ages and much of it was covered in snow and ice sheets. As the glaciers moved down from the high country and across the lowlands they scoured the rock surfaces, transporting great quantities of debris, both on top and within the ice sheet (glacial moraine) and dragged along underneath (glacial till). When the glaciers finally reached the sea they broke up into icebergs. They, in turn, would have carried the debris out to sea and dumped it on the sea floor.

This material, then, was deposited on the sea floor off the Gondwana coast: on the continental shelf and on the continental slope, and in the submarine trench along the subduction zone.

As the floor of the Pacific Ocean descended under the eastern edge of Gondwana the piles of sediment were scraped off the sea floor and stacked up in a series of overlapping sheets like pastry. However, each sheet was up to five kilometres thick! Eventually all this material 'gummed up' the subduction zone, as it were, and it had to do a sideways step towards the ancient ocean to by-pass all the accumulated material that, being lighter than the descending sea floor, could not be dragged downwards into the mantle, but kept on popping up like a cork floating in water. This enormous mass of folded and stacked sediment became attached (or 'accreted') to the eastern margin of Gondwana. Its weight must have been prodigious, so heavy in fact that the very crust of the earth bowed and sagged, unable to support its load.

There is obviously a limit to this process — the crust just can't keep on sinking forever. Sooner or later forces within the earth will combine to restore the balance and land will be pushed up above the sea. This 'uplifting' is partly helped by internal changes within the sediments.

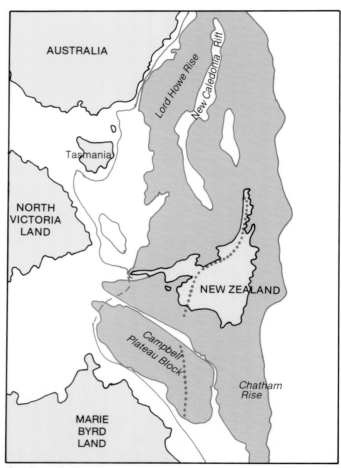

Continental New Zealand 135 million years ago.

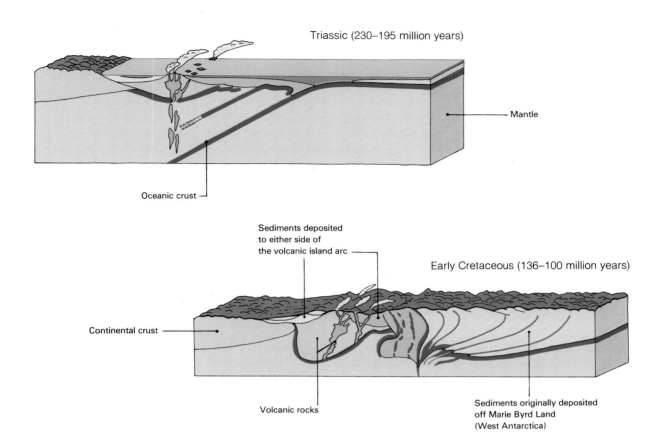

Triassic (230–195 million years)

Mantle

Oceanic crust

Sediments deposited
to either side of
the volcanic island arc

Early Cretaceous (136–100 million years)

Continental crust

Volcanic rocks

Sediments originally deposited
off Marie Byrd Land
(West Antarctica)

With the passage of time the layers of sediment will be compacted and their water content squeezed out of them by the sheer weight of the layers above. Also, the further down you go into the earth's crust the hotter it gets. This combination of heat and pressure will tend to lighten the rocks. Eventually, as more and more rocks are lightened in this way, the forces pushing the sediments deeper are neutralised and land will rise above the sea — no doubt helped by the buckling movements occurring anyway along an active continental margin.

The rocks created during this time now form the backbone of New Zealand and make up about two-thirds of the land rocks. They are collectively termed the Torlesse greywacke rocks (named after Canterbury's Mt Torlesse). The most common Torlesse rocks are light grey sandstones and black mudstones formed from sands and muds eroded from the adjacent Gondwana lands and carried by submarine landslides into the deep sea trench of the subduction zone. Less common in the Torlesse rocks are scraps of oceanic volcanic rock (basalt) caught up in the scraping of the oceanic plate. Often associated with these volcanic rocks are small patches of red and green argillite, chert and limestone sea-floor material rich in the various chemical components given off during the violent reactions between the cold sea water and the hot volcanic lava. Beds of conglomerates (layers of consolidated pebbles and gravels) also occasionally occur in Torlesse rocks. They and rare beds of mudstone fragments have been derived from older Torlesse sediments that have been compacted and then eroded

by wave action. This derived material has often slid down the continental slope to end up in the trench.

While the Torlesse sediments were in the subduction zones they were periodically joined by far-travelled fragments of exotic rocks (terranes) that had often originated in tropical regions far to the north and had been rafted for great distances southwards by sea-floor spreading movements. These exotic fragments, being lighter than the ocean floor on which they were riding, would not travel down into the subduction zone, but rather were scraped off and ended up being mixed into the Torlesse sediments already accumulating in the subduction zone. Thus, fragments of 'exotic' or 'displaced' terranes can be identified within stretches of country that are otherwise composed of Torlesse rocks.

The new land rose out of the sea during a period of mountain-building that is called the Rangitata Orogeny (derived from *oros* = mountain and the Rangitata River, draining the eastern flanks of the central Southern Alps). It was during this time that the rocks now forming the cores of most of the mountainous regions of New Zealand were first raised above the sea. During these mountain-building movements segments of the ancient sea floor were caught up, torn into slices, turned upside down, and thrust into and pushed over sediments that became part of the new landmasses. Today, these sediments, containing fossilised seashells, can be seen in what have become hills and mountains many hundreds of metres high.

albeit well-watered, for their journey to New Zealand. Today, three living species of native frog are known, all belonging to the genus *Leiopelma*. Considered the most primitive living frogs in the world, they are virtually the same frogs that are known as fossils from rocks of late Jurassic age.

Not surprisingly, they have retained some primitive features, among which is the presence of tail-wagging muscles (although they have no tail!). Another vestige of their past is the absence of ear-drums or vocal sacs, which means that they can only manage a rather un-froglike thin high-pitched squeak. They also lack any webbing between the toes and hind feet. But perhaps the most fascinating thing about them is their life history. Unlike most frogs, they do not have a free-swimming tadpole stage and all development takes place within a gelatinous capsule derived from the egg originally laid by the female. Because of this, *Leiopelma* is not tied to pools and streams, as most frogs are, and can inhabit a large range of forest environments.

Old beak head

Although externally similar to many lizards, the tuatara has several primitive features which place it apart from other reptilian orders. It is the only remaining member of the Order Rhynchocephalia (beak-headed) and can be justifiably called a living fossil for it has survived without modification for the best part of 200 million years. In all parts of the world except New Zealand, other members of this order became extinct and only on the islands of

ABOVE LEFT AND ABOVE: *Tuatara hatchlings and the adult tuatara (*Sphenodon punctatus). *Until a few hundred years ago tuataras lived on the mainland and ranged from North Cape to Bluff. Now, however, they are restricted to off-shore islands in the Auckland–Coromandel–Bay of Plenty region and Cook Strait.* TOP RIGHT: *The giant native land snail,* Paryphanta. ABOVE RIGHT: *The caterpillar-like* Peripatus.

New Zealand, isolated for at least the last 100 million years, did the tuatara survive.

It is a powerfully built, rather awkward animal capable of reaching a length of 60 centimetres. The name tuatara is Maori for 'spines on the back' and refers to the crest of elongated moveable horny spines along the neck and back. The skull, ribs and backbone all have primitive features that hark back to the 'stem reptiles' of the Permian and Triassic (that is, the group from which all reptiles are presumed to have descended). Perhaps the most notable feature is the presence of a vestigial 'third eye' apparent on the top of the head in young tuataras, but becoming covered over in adults. In other respects the tuatara is quite distinct from other reptiles. Whereas most reptiles reach a peak of activity when the body temperature is between 25°C and 38°C, the tuatara performs best at 12°C–17°C — the lowest requirement for warmth in all the reptiles and undoubtedly a factor which enabled its survival in New Zealand's temperate climate. Accordingly, bodily processes and growth rates are relatively slow and tuataras may live for more than 100 years.

A 'missing link'

Another animal that probably crossed from Gondwana in Jurassic times to populate the primaeval New Zealand forest was the ancestor of the worm caterpillar *Peripatus*. *Peripatus* is a member of a very ancient group of animals (the Phylum Onychophora — or 'claw bearers') which have existed from the middle of the Cambrian period, some 550 million years ago. All have a body divided, rather like that of an earthworm, into many segments which cannot be seen from the outside. Each segment bears a pair of small stumpy legs with two tiny claws.

From the time of its discovery, *Peripatus* has been regarded as something of a biological oddity. Because of its unusual anatomy its affinities with other invertebrate groups were in the past rather confused. Now, however, it is recognised as the 'missing link' between the segmented worms (Phylum Annelida) and the jointed-legged invertebrates such as crayfish, wood-lice and so on (Phylum Arthropoda).

The New Zealand *Peripatus* is a small, greyish-green, velvet-skinned caterpillar-like animal commonly found under logs and rocks in the bush. It is a nocturnal hunter and feeds on a wide range of small animals such as springtails, termites and insect larvae. It uses a unique method to capture food: when faced with a likely meal, it raises its head and squirts a stream of slime emitted from glands on either side of its mouth. On contact with the air the slime thickens and hardens, becoming incredibly strong, falling over the victim like a net. The *Peripatus* then moves in and by means of its jaws cuts a neat hole in the body wall and sucks the prey dry.

Native earthworms

Even the lowly earthworm is yet another remnant of the original Gondwana forest life. Not, however, the ordinary worms in your garden — these have been introduced — but rather the less common native worms, including the milk worm (or Maori worm), which can exceed 300 millimetres in length, and the spectacular North Auckland worm *Spenceriella gigantea*. This worm, New Zealand's largest, reaches an amazing 1.4 metres in length and 11 millimetres in width. Its burrows are often 20 millimetres in diameter and have been found still continuing downward at a depth of 3.5 metres.

Some 173 native worm species still survive, mainly confined to areas of native forest. Although some of these species are related to Australian worms, many of them also have relatives in southern South America, the Falklands, southern South Africa and New Caledonia as well as Australia. Although most earthworms can live for some time in fresh water, most are unable to pass even a narrow arm of salt water. Worm cocoons are laid below the surface of the earth and are normally inaccessible to birds and other animals and it is unlikely that birds would transport either worms or cocoons in mud caked on their legs. Like the frog, we again have to seek the origin of such a distribution pattern back when Gondwana was in existence and terrestrial creatures could move freely across continuous land.

Insect rodents and snails

A striking feature of the present New Zealand insect life

35

Among the endemic animal species to migrate to New Zealand from Gondwana during the Jurassic were the ancestors of: (A) the weta, (B) the snails Paryphanta *and* Wainuia, *(C) at least three species of frogs, (D)* Peripatus, *(E) the ratites, (F) the tuatara.*

is the considerable number and variety of large flightless ground-surface insects — many of which have relatives only in those countries that were once part of southern Gondwana.

Perhaps the most notable of the flightless insects are the unusual giant giraffe weevils (*Lasiorhynchus barbicornis*), included among the first animals to be described from New Zealand by J. C. Fabricius in 1775, and the wetas (*Deinacrida, Hemideina*). Wetas, which have the appearance of giant flightless crickets but with a fearsome array of spikes and prominent jaws, have a long fossil history and related forms have been found in rocks of Triassic age (about 200 million years old) from Queensland. Ancestors of the wetas may well have migrated here about this time when land routes were probably at their best. After New Zealand became isolated, and in the absence of terrestrial mammals, the wetas developed habits and lifestyles similar to those of small rodents. Wetas, like mice and rats, hole up during the day and emerge at night to roam the forest floor. As they feed on vegetation and forest floor debris, they produce rodent-like droppings. As such the rat-sized giant weta (*Deinacrida*) has been called an 'insect rodent'. It is the world's heaviest insect and weighs about 68 grams — the average weight of a thrush. Once fairly widespread in the North Island lowlands, the giant weta became extinct throughout most areas during the early days of European settlement, probably as a result of the spread of and predation by the European rat. Recently a colony of giant wetas has been found in an isolated back-country area covering several hectares south of Te Kuiti. Until then, the giant weta was believed to be confined to two small pockets in the South Island and four rat-free offshore islands. The Te Kuiti enclave managed to avoid extinction by adapting its lifestyle until the wetas spend most of their time living just under the canopy of gorse bushes, feeding at night and resting during the day among the dead debris in the bushes — so avoiding ground-level predation from rodents.

Like the weta, New Zealand's largest native snails also show traces of their Gondwana heritage. One group, including *Paryphanta* and *Wainuia*, have coiled shells up to 110 millimetres in diameter, and studies suggest that they belong to the oldest family of land snails, having originated in the late Palaeozoic or early Mesozoic. These land snails probably came to New Zealand at about the same time as the native frog and tuatara and have survived in isolation, whereas elsewhere the original ancestral lineages have given way to others that have produced the ubiquitous European snail (*Helix aspersa*), the bane of many a gardener's life.

BELOW: *The head of a tree weta. In the absence of terrestrial mammals wetas developed to occupy the same niche as small rodents.* BELOW RIGHT: Leiopelma archeyi *tailed froglets in their gelatinous capsules.* BOTTOM RIGHT: *The rare Hamilton's frog, now restricted to two offshore islands in Cook Strait and Pelorus Sound.*

The early birds

Yet another early migrant at this time would have been the newly evolved ancestors of the birds. These evolved from reptiles but it is not clear *which* reptile! The well-known group of flying reptiles called pterosaurs has nothing whatever to do with birds, fossil or otherwise. Although pterosaurs flew, they probably specialised in gliding rather than in flapping flight. Their wing structure was entirely different, just a web of skin supported by an enormously elongated fourth finger running along the rest of the arm and the side of the body to the thigh. Above all, they lacked that most diagnostic of all bird characteristics: the presence of feathers.

The first record of birds, or near-birds, is in rocks of later Jurassic age, 140 million years ago. At this time in a quiet shallow tropical lagoon in southern Germany, a number of remains of the early bird *Archaeopteryx* were preserved in very fine-grained limy muds on the lagoon floor. These sediments were so fine-grained that they were able to preserve the delicate impressions of feathers. The presence of feathers indicates clearly that the creature was a bird, or bird-like, because otherwise so many of its other features are like those of a small carnivorous theropod dinosaur. The similarities are so strong that some researchers regard birds as dinosaurs!

Despite the controversy about origins, it can be said that the crow-sized *Archaeopteryx* was well on its way to becoming a bird. It had feathers on a structural 'wing' and on an expanded tail. These 'flight' feathers were highly expanded in comparison with those on the

RM

RM

GR

remainder of the body and were undoubtedly of aerodynamic quality.

The descendants of *Archaeopteryx* radiated throughout the world and began to occupy many important ecological niches. One notable group of these early birds was the ratites. All ratites are characterised by the absence of a keel on the breast bone, to which the large wing muscles are attached in birds that fly (hence the origin of the name, derived from the Latin *ratis*: a raft or flat-bottomed boat, referring to the fact that ratite birds have a large, flattened, keel-less breast bone).

Besides the moas and kiwis of New Zealand, the ratites include the ostriches of Africa, the extinct elephant birds of Madagascar, the fossil ratite *Sylvornis* of New Caledonia, rheas of southern South America, emus of Australia and cassowaries of New Guinea and Australia.

Once it was thought that the ratites had diverged

Although both Archaeopteryx *and pterosaurs evolved from reptilian stock during the Mesozoic, they were unrelated. The descendants of* Archaeopteryx *evolved to become the modern birds.*

from the ancestral stock before birds had acquired the power of flight but because ratites show so many affinities with flying birds, it is now believed that they arose from flying ancestors whose wings and breast muscles degenerated once they increased in size and began to depend on their running ability to escape predators. The various ratite birds, although now widely separated geographically, are at the same time so similar that they must already have been flightless before being dispersed among the southern continents. Everything points to the probability that the ancestors of moas walked into New Zealand before it became isolated from the other Gondwana countries.

These ancestors probably originated in South America. The tinamous that live today in some parts of Central and South America are thought to have split off from the ratite group at about this time. Subsequently, the ancestral ratites lost their power of flight and soon after ratite groups became fairly widely distributed across Gondwana. One early group made its way from South America, across West Antarctica and into New Zealand, there to eventually produce the moas — our most fabulous fauna, now unfortunately extinct. Our living ratite, the kiwi, came later in Eocene times, about 40 million years ago, probably by flying across the infant Tasman Sea.

Archaeopteryx — Only the presence of feathers distinguishes *Archaeopteryx* as a bird. Like the pterosaur, it lacked a breast keel and was almost certainly a poor flier — suggested by the claws on its wings, used to snatch holds when gliding to a landing.

Pterosaur — The recent discovery of a pterosaur bone in the Hawke's Bay region confirms that pterosaurs were present in New Zealand for at least some time during the Mesozoic.

3. Land adrift

During the Cretaceous Period, some 80 million years ago, new sea floor formed to the west and south, rafting the ancestral landmass away from the rest of Gondwana and severing the links that had earlier channelled the mass migrations. New Zealand's long isolation had begun.

JURASSIC	CRETACEOUS	Paleocene
135 m.y.a.		65 m.y.a.

BY the early Cretaceous Period continuing earth movements had built up the ancestral New Zealand landmass into a continent of truly massive proportions so that for the first and only time in its history New Zealand rivalled Australia in size. The immense buckling, shearing and thrusting movements of the Rangitata Orogeny that had formed this landmass had created a topography every bit as varied as that of today, sustaining a rich diversity of lifeforms. Beds of fossil plants dating from this time at Huriwai Stream, on the coastline south of Port Waikato, contain beautifully preserved ferns and horsetails as well as leaves, cones and the stems of pine-like trees. These plants lived on a large river delta, built out into the head of a bay. Ferns colonised abandoned river channels, swamps and stream banks while coniferous forests grew on the more stable areas, which were nevertheless prone to flooding from adjacent overflowing river channels. Elsewhere in New Zealand, notably in Nelson and the West Coast, pollen-bearing sediments give us further glimpses of a forest-clad landscape.

It is believed that about this time in the early Cretaceous ancestors of the modern protea group of plants came to New Zealand from South America, using a southern route via western Antarctica. Proteas probably also moved into Australia and South Africa at the same time and eventually developed on these continents to produce the magnificent variety of proteas seen today. In New Zealand, by contrast — probably as a result of the ravages of succeeding ice ages — the protea group is today represented by only two rather inconspicuous plants: rewarewa (New Zealand honeysuckle *Knightia excelsa*) and toru (*Toronia toru*).

Having reached this vast size, why then was the ancestral New Zealand landmass not able to sustain its size, but instead became susceptible to erosion so that during the next 70 million years of the Cretaceous Period it was steadily reduced in both height and extent until by the end of that period it occupied an area only half its former size?

Once a mountainous terrain is thrust up by earth movements it is immediately attacked by fast-flowing rivers and streams and, if high enough, also by the effects of frost, snow and ice. The scree-strewn slopes and debris-laden rivers of the Southern Alps today provide eloquent testimony to the sheer power and intensity of the forces of erosion now attacking the country of New Zealand.

That erosion is calculated at a rate of some 2-6 millimetres per year — the amount of material being stripped off the high country. If it was not for the fact that the land itself is presently experiencing a period of sustained uplift, going back 3 million years and calculated at some 6-10 millimetres per year, then our majestic Southern Alps would have been reduced to low hills a long time ago rather like the eroded stumps of the mountain ranges of Australia. Obviously, substantial and continuous uplift is needed merely to keep ahead.

In the same way the Rangitata Orogeny during the Cretaceous gradually petered out, its force spent. In its wake it left towering outcrops of exposed Torlesse muds and sands, themselves greatly weakened by the shearing and thrusting of the uplift. These rocks were now attacked by the agents of erosion so that by the close of the Cretaceous, 70-65 million years ago, much of the ancestral landmass was at a low level with sea steadily encroaching along the east coasts of both islands. Many environments either disappeared or underwent drastic alteration. High country habitats progressively disappeared, giving way to habitats more typical of alluvial plains, and coastal habitats were steadily encroached upon by the sea, which eventually destroyed or modified them.

And yet despite the deleterious impact such erosion had on the landscape, the Cretaceous was also a period of surprising diversity, of increasing sophistication in the biota that migrated to New Zealand and that was to culminate in the evolution of flowering plants (angiosperms). It was also a period of great global change, which we suspect was at some point cataclysmic.

The end of the balmy days

As the Jurassic Period drew to a close the first almost imperceptible movements occurred along the sites of the modern South Atlantic and Indian Oceans that were to lead ultimately to the wholesale dismemberment of Gondwana. These movements took the form of the opening up of lines of steadily widening splits, separating Western Gondwana (South America, Africa, Arabia, Malagasy and India) from Eastern Gondwana (Antarctica, Australia, New Guinea, New Caledonia and New Zealand).

As Gondwana broke up, sea poured into the gaps left between the emergent continents. Where Antarctica and India separated from Africa the embryonic Indian

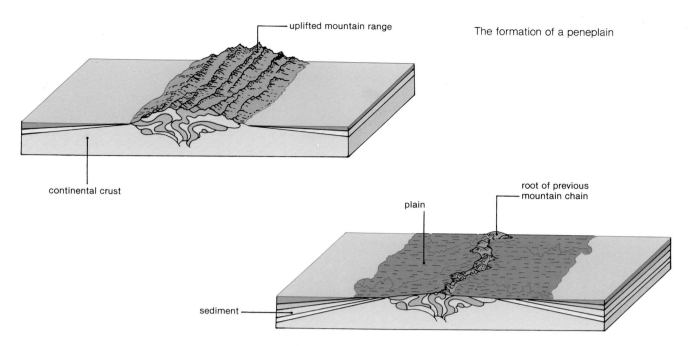

uplifted mountain range

The formation of a peneplain

continental crust

root of previous mountain chain

plain

sediment

The new landmass created by the Rangitata Orogeny was attacked by erosion and progressively levelled, the eroded material being deposited in the sea. By middle and late Cretaceous time, 100–65 million years ago, a peneplain had formed.

Ocean was formed; similarly, where South America and Africa separated the South Atlantic Ocean was formed. By middle Cretaceous times the global patterns of land and sea and mountain ranges as we know them today began to be roughed out for the first time. Major movements of the continents were underway, and as a result oceanic areas were either actively widening (the Atlantic and Indian Oceans), or going through a preliminary cracking and splitting phase (rifting), before pulling apart.

In the South-West Pacific other changes were underway — the climate was cooling. From late Jurassic times onwards the opening up of the oceanic gaps in Western Gondwana had the effect of swinging Eastern Gondwana towards the South Pole, reversing the rotation of Triassic and Jurassic times. As a result, the geographic position of New Zealand changed from 55°S latitude in late Jurassic times to about 85°S latitude in the middle Cretaceous. New Zealand now lay virtually on the South Pole but because there were no major landmasses in that vicinity, there was probably no polar ice nor frigid polar climatic zones. Like those of the Triassic and Jurassic periods, the widths of the other climatic zones were much broader than those of today and cool- to cold-temperate climates prevailed in the regions in which New Zealand now found itself.

And then at the close of the early Cretaceous the first signs of movements that eventually were to split New Zealand away from Australia began on the site of the modern Tasman Sea. Long split-like rift valleys developed along the western margin of New Zealand, along the Lord

Howe Rise and the eastern margin of Australia (at this time all in close contact). As these valleys deepened and became more extensive the sea flooded in, forming long finger-like marine embayments — the precursors of the Tasman Sea.

Rifting was, however, only part of the picture. As we know, the ancestral New Zealand landmass was being rapidly eroded by rivers and weathering so that by 110 millions years ago the land in many areas had either been worn down to sea level or had been flooded by the sea. The combined effects of rifting and erosion now meant that the land links to the north and west that had earlier channelled the mass migrations of plant and animal species to New Zealand were broken. Between Australia and New Zealand lay the nascent Tasman Sea, posing a barrier which succeeding species would find difficult to cross. Enter the angiosperm.

The rise of the flowering plants

As New Zealand drifted away from Australia, it carried on its landscape populations of ancient ferns, araucarian pines and podocarps that were then abundant in Gondwana. At this time, in middle Cretaceous, some 100 million years ago, new plants were appearing that were to achieve the acme of plant development. These plants, that were to develop into the flowering plants of today, are called the angiosperms. Like mammals, they have been enormously successful and have great powers of reproduction and survival. To survive winter non-woody perennial types die down to their roots in autumn and sprout new shoots in spring while trees discard their leaves and become dormant. But it is the flower that is the most important and unique angiosperm structure. Reproductively more efficient than the separate male and female cones of the conifers, the flower usually contains both pollen (male) and ovules (female), and may be pollinated

either by wind, or by insects it attracts (by colour, perfume or nectar), or even by itself.

In the middle and late Cretaceous angiosperms evolved and spread rapidly throughout the world, but on reaching the eastern shores of Australia they found the infant Tasman Sea blocking their passage to New Zealand. Nonetheless, judging from our records of fossil pollen, New Zealand did receive some of these early angiosperms soon after they first appeared. Just how they arrived can only be surmised — such are the vagaries of chance dispersal. Seeds may have been borne by winds or on logs that drifted across the narrow sea to be washed up on the shores of New Zealand — we do not know. What is more surprising is that some angiosperms, not so well endowed for dispersal, nevertheless still managed to get here. The southern beech is one such species that is very poorly equipped for trans-oceanic travel, and its presence here was for a long time a scientific enigma.

The New Zealand beech species belong to the genus *Nothofagus* ('false beech') of the family Fagacae which also includes the well-known Northern Hemisphere *Fagus* (the true beech), as well as the oak and chestnut. *Nothofagus* species are restricted to the Southern Hemisphere and so are often known as the 'southern beeches'. Species occur in New Guinea, New Caledonia, eastern Australia, Tasmania, southern South America and New Zealand. Fossil wood and pollen suggest that in the past southern beeches also populated Antarctica and Western Australia although there is no record of them, however, in South Africa or Madagascar.

The question that haunted scientists for so long was how could it have arrived in New Zealand? Its seeds sink quickly in water and die if exposed to salt water. That makes it impossible for the seeds to float across the ocean or be transported on floating logs since splashing by salt water would kill them. *Nothofagus* seeds also cannot withstand freezing, making transport by floating ice equally unlikely. The seeds are not attractive to birds, making bird transport also unlikely. Finally, *Nothofagus* is not easily spread by wind; after the deforestation of the Ice Age, the southern beech did not re-establish itself on Stewart Island (32 kilometres off New Zealand) nor on Great Barrier Island, a mere 18 kilometres from the nearest seed source.

Obviously, *Nothofagus* needs virtually continuous land for its distribution, and because of this many of the early botanists postulated extensive land bridges spanning the southern oceans and connecting the lands now forested with *Nothofagus*. Since then continental drift has provided a more probable mechanism to achieve such dispersal without the need to cross oceans. As far as New Zealand is concerned, the major conclusion we can draw from the *Nothofagus* story is that although Australia and New Zealand may well have been separated by the time these plants arrived on the scene, New Zealand was still linked to Antarctica and South America, and that such links persisted for some time after the Tasman started to open. These links must also have been extensive because other plants, equally poorly endowed for dispersal, accompanied *Nothofagus* on its southerly route. They included members of the Magnolia, Protea and Fuschia families — many of which grace our forests and gardens today.

LLOYD HOMER

The Poolburn–Rough Ridge area of Central Otago, east of Cromwell. Central Otago today provides the most continuous and best preserved remnant of the ancient peneplain laid down over 80 million years ago.

BELOW: *In the Southern Hemisphere 120 million years ago sea-floor spreading had commenced in the South Atlantic between Africa and South America. By 90 million years ago rifting had separated South Africa, Malagasy, India and Australia, and sea-floor spreading had commenced in the Indian Ocean between India and Antarctica.*

120 million years ago

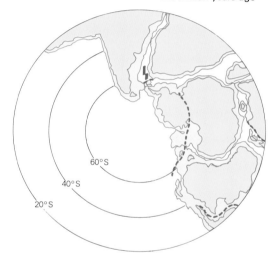

The overall impression we are left with is that during the middle Cretaceous continuous forest probably extended throughout Gondwana, linking South America to Antarctica and Antarctica to New Zealand and Australia. Today we are reminded of this by its vestiges separated by thousands of kilometres. It is uncanny to note that the *Nothofagus* forests of New Zealand and South America resemble each other so closely that each has the same parasitic fungi, mosses and flightless sucking bugs inhabiting their bark — suggesting that one continuous southern forest once linked the two countries.

And yet, within a few million years all this was to change.

Birth of the Tasman Sea

During the late Cretaceous (95–65 million years ago) the Atlantic and Indian Oceans continued to open at a steady rate. India pulled away from Gondwana to begin its long journey northwards to join Asia, and Malagasy pulled away from Africa. These and other opening movements around the southern sectors of Gondwana now had the effect of rotating Eastern Gondwana northwards away from the South Pole. In the New Zealand region this culminated about 80 million years ago in the appearance of open ocean in the Tasman Sea and, more crucially, to the south of New Zealand. Where once virtually continuous land had linked New Zealand to Antarctica, channelling a succession of land migrants spanning nearly 100 million years, now open sea conditions prevailed.

90 million years ago

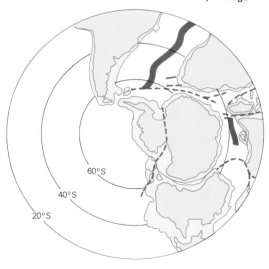

New Zealand had effectively been cut off from the rest of Gondwana.

We know this because in the late Cretaceous ancestral marsupials probably spread from South America to Australia, presumably by using Antarctica as a stepping stone, but apparently were not able to reach New Zealand. Their entry into New Zealand was barred by the stretches of open sea then present in the Tasman, South-West Pacific, and Southern Ocean.

The marsupials (or pouched animals) include opossums, koalas, wombats and kangaroos. Today they are found in abundance only in Australia, although opossums are found in North America, and opossums and selvas in South America. Fossil marsupials are known from these countries as well as Western Europe, North Africa and West Antarctica, suggesting that they were formerly more widespread but were progressively replaced by other more advanced mammals. Although they are otherwise efficient animals, in terms of their reproductive systems marsupials may be considered to represent an early stage of mammal development. Young marsupials are born at a very early stage and crawl into the mother's pouch, where they become attached to a teat and continue growth. In the more advanced 'placental' mammals this development of the young is internal, in a uterus or womb, nourished by a placenta.

The egg-laying monotremes (platypus and echidna) are even more primitive and can be viewed as being one step removed from reptiles. They had originally migrated to Australia in early Cretaceous times, probably by using the same southern land routes that the protea had used to enter New Zealand. The intriguing question is, if proteas were able to enter both Australia and New Zealand during the early Cretaceous, why then were the ancestral monotremes only able to gain entry to Australia but not New Zealand? Fundamental differences may have existed in the routes available to the proteas compared with those available to the monotremes. For example, the route to New Zealand across West Antarctica probably favoured organisms with cool or cold-temperate requirements and for this reason may not have been particularly attractive to the early monotremes. On the other hand, the route the monotremes took to Australia probably used East Antarctica as a stepping stone, which may have had a warmer, possibly subtropical climate. Having reached Australia, the monotremes were, of course, prevented from migrating to New Zealand by the embryonic Tasman Sea, which made land migration to New Zealand all but impossible.

Nevertheless, it is the failure of the marsupials to migrate to New Zealand during late Cretaceous times that effectively marks the beginning of New Zealand's isolation. Certainly, terrestrial migration from Gondwana and Antarctica was no longer possible. The reptiles and ratites that had earlier migrated to New Zealand would now evolve independently of outside influences, their development only responding to the demands of their local environment. That does not mean to say that all land lifeforms were prevented from migrating to New Zealand, only those that travelled along the ground. Birds and seed carried by the wind could still traverse the narrow seas to the west and south to populate New Zealand.

(Continued on page 48.)

*The southern beech (*Nothofagus*) is today distributed widely throughout the Southern Hemisphere, suggesting that once continuous land linked countries now separated by thousands of kilometres of sea.*

RM

MESOZOIC FLORA

MESOZOIC fossils of land plants, consisting primarily of leaves, woody stems, roots, hard seeds and fruits, are often found in terrestrial sediments and less often as material that has been floated in and incorporated into marine sediments. These fossils, visible to the naked eye (and called 'macrofossils'), are obvious but many people do not realise that the most abundant fossil plants consist of minute spores and pollen which are very common throughout terrestrial and marine sedimentary rocks. These microfossils, usually 30–60 microns in size (1 micron = 1/1000 millimetre), are produced in great quantities by most plants and are dispersed by wind, water, birds, insects or other animals. Fossils of this size cannot be seen by the naked eye. The more fragile and ephemeral parts of plants, like flowers, are only rarely preserved, providing a difficult exercise in reconstructing the original plant from all the possible preservable parts.

The Triassic period was generally dry and warm and the fossil plants reflected this by developing thick cuticles, protective waxy coatings to the leaves, and small, much divided leaflets. The most common Triassic plants, found throughout New Zealand, were the seed-ferns — fern-like plants producing seeds like the conifers rather than spores like the true ferns. Of these *Dicroidium* was the most abundant, producing a remarkable variety of forms, all characterised by forked fronds and separate pollen- and seed-bearing fronds. During this period the conifers, cycads and ginkgos evolved and diversified and adapted to the drier climate. Cycads are palm-like plants characterised today by very large cones, often the size of rugby balls; ginkgos are a special group of conifers that produce broad fan-shaped leaves on dwarf branches.

These plants dominated the Triassic forests, forming the emergent trees, while the low shrub and ground cover was dominated by *Dicroidium*, other seed-ferns, lycopods, horsetails, tree-ferns, ground ferns, mosses and liverworts. Fossils of the bryophytes (mosses, hornworts, liverworts) are known only from spores which were so abundant

during the Mesozoic as to suggest that they were far more common and a far more important element of the vegetation than they are today.

An interesting locality, near Benmore Dam, southern Canterbury, contains a seaweed, *Shonabellia*, of the algal family Codiaceae, closely associated with two species of seed-fern called *Pachydermophyllum*. It is likely that *Pachydermophyllum* grew in coastal situations along inland reaches of estuaries occupying the same habitat as the mangrove *Avicennia* does today in northern New Zealand. A reconstruction of the middle Triassic New Zealand landscape extending from the coastline inland suggests green codiacean algae growing on rocky coastal outcrops, *Pachydermophyllum* 'mangroves' on river flats near the sea and broadleaf woodlands further inland dominated by ferns, seed-ferns and rarer conifers, ginkgos and cycads. Because of the deciduous nature of the plants (i.e. dropping leaves in winter), and the low numbers of species, it has been argued that, although the climate was generally dry and warm, at Benmore at least the middle Triassic climate was cool-temperate and seasonally snowy, but not so cold as to inhibit the growth of trees.

The abundance of leaves, wood and pollen grains in the Jurassic and Cretaceous indicates that the forests of these periods were dominated by diverse cycads and conifers often forming dense forests, some now preserved *in situ* (for example, Curio Bay, Southland). The seed-ferns, so dominant in the Triassic, became extinct and in their place ferns, especially tree-ferns, became more prominent. One of the most abundant fossil ferns of the Jurassic was *Cladophlebis*, often called the Mesozoic weed because of its abundance. *Cladophlebis* is the frond of an osmundaceous fern and today the New Zealand Osmundaceae is represented only by *Todea* and *Leptopteris*.

Many unrelated Mesozoic species shared common characteristics. For example, *Pentoxylon*, the wood of a characteristic Jurassic and early Cretaceous plant that produced large fleshy fruits in loose cones, may be found at Waikato Heads. It bore a very common and charac-

Jurassic plant fossils (Clent Hills, Canterbury).

LEFT: *The flowers of the rewarewa are like those of no other native plant. Although they conform to the flower patterns of other protea, there are no petals and instead the 30 to 50 flowers are densely packed into a 100mm long raceme — the effect is of a floral 'pin cushion'.* ABOVE: *The flowers of the southern beech,* Nothofagus.

teristic leaf called *Taeniopteris*; the fruit is known as *Carnoconites*. The plant was probably a rather floppy, flexible shrub. An extinct group of conifers called the Bennettitales also produced *Taeniopteris*-like leaves, suggesting that identical leaves could be produced by totally unrelated plants.

Most pieces of fossil wood found in the Jurassic and Cretaceous rocks have annual rings indicating a seasonal, temperate climate and a moist environment.

The Cretaceous was a time of great change in the vegetation when the ginkgos, cycads and conifers generally declined in importance or became extinct at the same time as the flowering plants evolved and became dominant. Nonetheless, two groups of conifers became reasonably common. These were the podocarps, ancestors of the modern totara, miro and matai, and the araucarians. Some fossil podocarps evolved that no longer grow in New Zealand, including the Huon pine, now restricted to temperate rainforests of western Tasmania. Although no macrofossils of the Huon pine (*Lagarostrobos franklinii*) have been recognised, its characteristic pollen is often the dominant pollen type in late Cretaceous pollen assemblages. Other pollen types are also abundant including *Microcachrys*, a genus also now restricted to Tasmania, *Podocarpus* and *Dacrydium cupressinum* (rimu), which appears towards the close of the Cretaceous. Araucarian leaves, resin, wood and pollen are often varied and abundant, the leaves often forming thick beds in some coal-bearing sequences such as those of Shag Point, Otago.

The low-lying landscape of the late Cretaceous provided the ideal setting for the development of peat swamps in which plants grew and died to form coal deposits. The vegetation that provided much of this coal was mainly podocarp and araucarian. Spores and pollen from ferns, bryophytes, horsetails, lycopods and angiosperms (flowering plants) are numerically less important, but the plants may nevertheless have been relatively common in the vegetation. Elsewhere, tree ferns were abundant, producing spores like the modern tree ferns *Cyathea* and *Dicksonia*. Lycopods, horsetails, ground ferns such as *Gleichenia* (umbrella fern) and hepatics are all found as macrofossils and microfossils.

The most important aspect of Cretaceous vegetation was the evolution of flowering plants from which most of our plant food is now obtained. The evolution of flowering plants is a mystery: we just do not know how angiosperms evolved and what group or groups of plants they evolved from. Flowers are not commonly preserved and those that have been are all of advanced forms and show no obvious connection to the fruiting bodies of any older plants. It is the flowers that provide the basis for classifying flowering plants. The net-like patterns on the leaves of flowering plants are also very characteristic but while other extinct groups of plants also have similar leaves, there is no obvious connection between these groups and the flowering plants. The most primitive angiosperm probably had a magnolia-like flower, and it is from a magnolia-like ancestor that all our flowering plants evolved. The first undisputed angiosperm macrofossils appeared in the early Cretaceous at about the same time all over the world, but some scientists believe that they must have existed in the Jurassic because the first macrofossils indicate that

ABOVE: *The floral structure of the modern* Magnolia *is believed to be similar to that of the early primitive angiosperms that developed some 100 million years ago.* RIGHT: Ascarina lucida *or hutu belongs to a family that was one of the first families of flowering plants to appear in New Zealand.*

angiosperms were already well advanced in their evolution. Distinctive angiosperm pollen, with its rod-like structure, and wide dispersal abilities, also first appeared in the early Cretaceous and these grains tend to be primitive in their morphology.

In New Zealand the earliest angiosperms appear in the middle Cretaceous. The fossil leaves are often large, simple, either with smooth entire margins or with coarse toothed serrate margins. Many of the leaves were asymmetrical, had diverse shapes and an irregular venation pattern. Such leaves may be found at Kyeburn, Central Otago, Pitt Island in the Chathams, and in the Clarence Valley at Quail Flat and Coverham. Although some leaves look superficially very similar to *Nothofagus* leaves, they cannot be identified or compared with any known flowering plants that exist today. The earliest floras contain no evidence of monocotyledonous plants (grasses, lilies, palms). All the early flowering plants were broadleafed and one large-leaved palm-like plant grew at Pakawau, north-west Nelson, in the late Cretaceous, producing leaves that were at least 4 metres long, similar but larger than the modern genus *Musa*, of the banana family.

Pollen of the earliest New Zealand angiosperms are very small, inconspicuous and most cannot be identified or compared with modern plants. However, one of the earliest pollen types is very similar to pollen of the New Zealand plant hutu or *Ascarina*, which suggests that the family to which it belongs must have been one of the first families of flowering plants to have appeared in New Zealand.

Once angiosperms appeared they quickly diversi-

fied and adapted to many different habitats so that by the end of the Cretaceous many modern plants, or at least their immediate ancestors, had appeared. Also by the late Cretaceous New Zealand had split off from Antarctica and Australia and our vegetation started evolving independently of the other southern continents, supplemented by occasional arrivals of plants with good dispersal capabilities.

By the end of the Cretaceous the proteas and southern beeches (*Nothofagus*) were common and varied. Other flowering plants to appear in the New Zealand late Cretaceous were the ancestors of the modern Caryophyllaceae (pinks), Cruciferae (wall flowers), Ericaceae (heaths, grass-trees), *Gunnera* (gunnera), *Ilex* (hollies), Liliaceae (lilies), Loranthaceae (mistletoes), Pseudowintera (pepper trees), Ranunculaceae (buttercups), Polypodiaceae (polypodiums). *Phyllocladus* (celery pines) and *Podocarpus* (totara) also appeared then.

Although many of New Zealand's modern plants are closely related to late Cretaceous and early Tertiary ancestors most endemic species evolved in New Zealand at a later stage in New Zealand's geological history.

Although the modern vegetation owes its origin to these ancestors, in no way should modern vegetation assemblages be regarded as relict Gondwana floras; they are in every sense of the word modern and owe their formation, development and current composition to the glaciations and concurrent climatic changes of the last 2 million years. Thus dinosaurs, for example, never roamed through podocarp forests similar to those that exist in New Zealand today, instead, the vegetation was almost totally composed of plants no longer in existence.

In this scene a pair of carnivorous theropods attack two hypsilophodonts. The four-metre-long theropod has been estimated at about 400 kilograms in weight. The bird-hipped hypsilophodont was a herbivore and probably lived in the forest margins.

The New Zealand Dinosaurs

As a result of the migrations of the mid-Jurassic some 150 million years ago, New Zealand received and sustained a diverse range of land animals, the remnants of which still live in our forests. However, until recently it was thought that we had been denied the dinosaur groups that spread far and wide elsewhere in the world.

Then from the mid-1970s a series of remarkable discoveries were made which have revolutionised our thinking about our land fauna during these times. After many years of patient work, an amateur palaeontologist, Joan Wiffen, assisted by her husband Pont, while exploring inland Hawke's Bay, found a small eight-centimetre bone which was later identified as a tailbone from a medium-sized, two-legged

carnivorous theropod. Its presence in marine sediment suggests the landform of that part of Hawke's Bay at that time, in the late Cretaceous, 70 million years ago — a broad, forested lowland with an estuarine coastline and shallow coastal waters. When the dinosaur died, its carcass was presumably swept into a nearby river or stream and washed out to sea to be deposited on the seabed.

The remains of this solitary predator remained an enigma for several years — but within a decade Joan had made further discoveries from the same site which balanced the picture of our land fauna then. We now know that both dinosaur groups — Ornithischia and Saurischia — were present here for at least part of the Mesozoic. These included both carnivores and

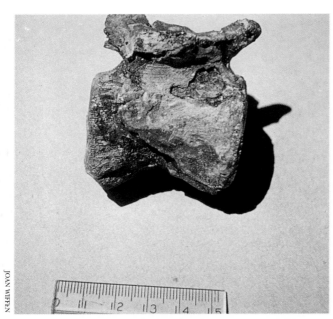

JOAN WIFFEN

The first New Zealand dinosaur to be correctly identified — a theropod — was identified from this single vertebral tail bone occurring in marine rocks deposited 70-65 million years ago and located in a tributary of the Te Hoe River, inland Hawke's Bay.

herbivores. Among the carnivores, two types have been found in the marine sediments of Hawke's Bay. Both stood on their hind legs and, to judge from the heavy musculature apparent in overseas specimens, must have been capable of moving swiftly. The smaller of the two is related to *Megalosaurus,* which typically was about 4 metres long and weighed about half a tonne. The larger is similar to *Allosaurus,* which was one of the major predators of North America and Australia. With its large head, ferocious teeth and curved claws, *Allosaurus* is the stuff of popular science, and overseas specimens reached an impressive 12 metres in length, stood 7-8 metres tall and weighed up to 2 tonnes.

To sustain adequate numbers of such predators the New Zealand fauna would have required a sizeable contemporary herbivore population. In New Zealand, these were represented by three vastly different types. The largest was a sauropod about the size of an elephant and weighing perhaps 3-4 tonnes. It may have lived in herds and it probably fed on the young leaves of forest trees, using its long neck to reach considerable heights, occasionally rearing up on its hind legs to stretch even higher.

To escape the predations of the carnivores, the herbivores developed two main mechanisms for defence: mobility and/or armour. The hypsiloph-odonts, of which at least one type is found in New Zealand, were small, lightly built dinosaurs of about 3 metres in length that could run very fast on their well-developed hind legs. They occupied the same niche as the antelopes and gazelles of the modern African veldt, feeding on the shrubby foliage of the forest margins where they lived. In North America they lived

in herds and, judging from the discovery of nesting sites in Montana, probably nested in colonies and were also likely to have provided care for their young after hatching, rather like modern birds.

The so-called armoured dinosaurs or ankylosaurs also lived here. Because the evidence is presently limited only to the partial remains of a rib bone and vertebrae, we don't yet know exactly what the New Zealand ankylosaur looked like, or to which genus or species it belonged. However, overseas ankylosaurs are small, four-footed, low-slung animals about the size of a small car. They were covered with armour plates and some had spines and others had bony plates with nodules, like chain mail, protecting the back of the neck. Their weak flattened teeth (for crushing and eating vegetation) and stubby claws were often more than compensated for by their powerful armoured tail, often edged with long, sharp spines and ending in a heavy club.

As exciting as these discoveries are, the intriguing question remains: where did they come from? Presently the evidence is too scanty for any definitive conclusions. Nevertheless two scenarios have emerged.

All the dinosaur fossils date from the same period — the late Cretaceous. Does this mean that New Zealand's dinosaurs only date from this period? Certainly, the climate then was more equable than during the early and middle Cretaceous, when New Zealand was virtually at the South Pole. However, by the late Cretaceous the land that previously linked New Zealand to the rest of Gondwana had disappeared. As we know, it was probably for this reason that the ancestral monotremes were not able to reach here. Everything points to the dinosaurs reaching New Zealand sometime during the Jurassic or early Cretaceous. The absence of land fossils from these times is undoubtedly due to the vagaries of fossilisation.

But where did our dinosaurs come from? At this point opinions diverge. One theory suggests Australia as the likely source, arguing that the southern land route followed by *Nothofagus* was too cold for the supposedly cold-blooded dinosaurs. The other theory points to the recent findings of dinosaurian remains in Antarctica, and argues that the dinosaurs, like the tuatara (also a reptile), most probably followed the southern land route through Antarctica. The route would have first been blazed by the vast *Nothofagus* forests because, logically, the herbivores would have followed a trail of suitable vegetation, and the carnivores would have pursued their prey.

A parade of marine life

If the appearance of dinosaurs in New Zealand during the late Cretaceous provided a highlight in the evolution of land fauna, so too did the waters surrounding our shores: they now teemed with marine life. In this, New Zealand shared in a worldwide phenomenon. The global movements underway throughout the Cretaceous were breaking up both Laurasia and Gondwana and cracks were appearing everywhere across the surfaces of the once

RIGHT: *An ammonite fossil of Jurassic age, 190–135 million years ago, (Te Puti, Kawhia),* ABOVE: *A preserved belemnite guard of Jurassic age, (Port Waikato). At Kawhia Harbour, pre-European Maoris believed such guards were the excrement of mullets.*

mighty super-continents. Some of the cracks were to open up to form the modern ocean basins. Other cracks did not get very far beyond stages similar to that of the modern East African rift valley system. In these instances, as the subterranean forces pulling them apart waned and eventually died out they became filled with lake and estuarine material, often very rich in organic matter, which with the passage of time has helped form extensive oil fields, such as those found today in the Niger Basin of West Africa.

Such splitting movements, as well as creating gaps into which the ocean could enter, also arched and rucked up large areas of the crust, forming systems of broadly domed mid-oceanic ridges, swollen by massive subterranean concentrations of magma, which in time welled up to form new sea floor. The sea water displaced by such domed mid-oceanic ridges was sent flooding across the edges of adjacent continents, resulting in environmental modifications on an enormous scale. As a result, global sea levels reached an all-time high during the middle and late Cretaceous and oceanic waters spread over large parts of North America, Africa and Europe. A broad seaway, up to 620 kilometres wide, traversed the length of the western interior of North America, extending from Alaska and Arctic Canada southwards some 2,000 kilometres to the Gulf of Mexico. In Africa sea covered North Africa and then moved across the Sahara, to link up with sea coming in from the South Atlantic across Nigeria and Chad. Sea also extended over much of western Europe and some 45 per cent of the present land area of the USSR was submerged. This came at a time when much of the land was low. With little

debris being eroded from the land into the sea, clear water conditions often prevailed, allowing sunlight to penetrate. And this, combined with the warm conditions, stimulated an enormous growth of microscopic marine algae.

These extensive areas of newly created, gently shelving continental platform proved fecund breeding grounds for marine life and during the late Cretaceous marine faunas were often exceedingly prolific and diverse.

In this New Zealand was no exception. Although the shallow marine links to the north and west had been severed by the deep sea basin of the Tasman Sea, strong marine links joining New Zealand and New Caledonia to South America via West Antarctica were still evident, enabling these countries to share a distinctive 'southern' marine fauna. Some elements of this fauna also extended to southern India, Malagasy and southern Africa. In the warm shallow shelf waters around our coasts, a dazzling variety of marine life thrived. Large coarsely ribbed clams (*Inoceramus*) — some exceeding a metre in width — were important members of the sea-floor community, as were a great variety of bivalves and gastropods. Other marine animals included nautiloids, sponges, corals, bryozoans, brachiopods, marine worms, scaphopods (tusk shells), crustaceans, barnacles, starfish, sea eggs and sea lilies. Turtle remains are known from Hawke's Bay, and sharks' teeth are common in many localities. (As the skeleton of a shark is composed of cartilage it is not normally preserved, and only the teeth remain as fossils.) Skeletons of bony fish and isolated fish scales are also known.

Some of the most bizarre marine animals in our waters at this time were the ammonites and belemnites. They were conspicuous members of the marine life in

During the late Cretaceous, 90–65 million years ago, a dazzling variety of marine life thrived in the waters around New Zealand. Although the nascent Tasman Sea had probably severed the shallow marine links to the north and west, New Zealand was still linked by shallow-water marine links to New Caledonia in the north and south America via West Antarctica to the south, enabling these countries to share a 'southern' marine fauna. Some elements of this also extended to southern India, Malagasy, and southern Africa.

Starfish — A group of echinoderms that have since Palaeozoic times resembled their modern forms.

Shark — Evolved during the late Devonian to dominate the seas during the Carboniferous, although they have maintained their diversity ever since.

many parts of the world, and in some areas of New Zealand they were more common than the various other types of shellfish. It is the abundance of their fossil record that has enabled us to describe in detail how they lived.

Ammonites and belemnites

Both groups were members of a class of animals called the Cephalopoda (a combination of words meaning 'head' and 'foot'). The name alludes to the fact that the molluscan 'foot' (the plough-like fleshy projection that bivalves such as the toheroa use to crawl or burrow on the sea floor) is in these animals united with the head and forms a ring of tentacles (often called 'arms') around the mouth. Another part of the foot forms a funnel, through which the animal can squirt out a jet of water (if necessary mixed with ink) and thus propel itself rapidly backward to escape danger.

The earliest cephalopods, in the Palaeozoic Era (570-230 million years ago), had a long narrow conical shell, the interior of which was divided into a series of chambers. At the open end of the cone was a large chamber (body chamber) in which the animal itself was accommodated, with its head and tentacles emerging. The other chambers were filled with gas and fluids which the animal could regulate and so adjust its level and position in the ocean, just like a submarine.

As geological time went by, forms evolved in which the conical chambered shell became coiled into a spiral, and this type still survives as the beautiful living animal called the pearly nautilus, an inhabitant of the tropical

seas of the West Pacific. Ammonites and *Nautilus* differ in the shape of the walls between successive chambers. In *Nautilus* the chamber wall forms a simple curve; in ammonites the chamber walls became complexly folded, providing support to the shell and allowing the ammonite to penetrate into deep or turbulent water without being crushed. As well, the outer side of the shell, smooth in *Nautilus*, was often in the ammonites richly ornamented with branched or unbranched ribbing, knobs and spikes and some forms have a rib-like keel along the outer edge of the shell.

Some ammonites resemble the spiral horn of a large ram and the whole group has been named after the Egyptian deity Ammon, who had the head of a ram. Abundant ammonites in the cliffs of Yorkshire — to the local people appearing to be like coiled-up snakes turned to stone — led to a legend identifying them with a plague of snakes quelled by Saint Hilda.

Generally, ammonites were not particularly large animals and most were between 50–200 millimetres in diameter, although giant forms are known. New Zealand's largest ammonite, from late Jurassic rocks south of Kawhia Harbour, is 1.52 metres in diameter. The largest ammonite known in the world is 2.55 metres in diameter and if uncoiled would have attained a massive length of 10.7 metres.

Most ammonites were probably good swimmers, but their diversity of form suggests that they lived in a wide variety of habitats. Some may have spent most of their life on or close to the sea floor; others may have floated in the sea, like *Nautilus*, and still others — the forms

Turtle — A northern migrant; turtle remains have been found in the Hawke's Bay region.

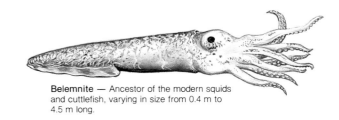

Belemnite — Ancestor of the modern squids and cuttlefish, varying in size from 0.4 m to 4.5 m long.

Brachiopod — Superficially similar to bivalves, brachiopods first appeared in the early Cambrian Era and were very common in the Palaeozoic and Mesozoic seas. They are less common today although still widespread throughout New Zealand waters.

Ammonite — ancestor of the modern *Nautilus*, and particularly prolific during the late Cretaceous when in some areas they were more common than the various other types of shellfish.

characterised by smooth streamlined shells — may have been energetic swimmers.

Ammonites were undoubtedly preyed upon by other sea dwellers. They could protect themselves by retracting the head and tentacles into the living chamber of the shell and closing off the open end by means of a plate, or two plates, similar to the periwinkle's 'cat's eye'. Nonetheless ammonite shells have been found that bear traces of injury scars where pieces of the shell, particularly close to the head, have been sliced out, presumably by biting predators. Large sharks abounded in the Mesozoic seas and probably were not averse to ammonite meals.

Belemnites, on the other hand, are thought to have been ancestors of present-day squids and cuttlefish. Certainly they looked and presumably acted like the modern squid. The body was torpedo-shaped and was surrounded by a fleshy mantle spreading out into two lateral fins that kept the body right side up and could be moved to guide it upward or downward. There was a constricted 'neck' behind the head, and the eyes, like those of the squid, were extremely efficient. Ten tentacles surrounded the mouth and were set with rows of strongly curved, sharp hooks (some of which are known from New Zealand rocks), for grasping and holding soft-bodied prey. Like most other cephalopods, belemnites had buoyancy chambers which they used to regulate the depth to which they sank. Also like other cephalopods, they probably swam by taking water into the mantle cavity and forcing it out as a jet through the funnel. When the funnel pointed forward, the belemnite moved backward; when it was pointed to the rear, the belemnite moved forward. Alarm would cause the animal to release a thick dark liquid from an ink sac that opened into the cavity and through the funnel. The ink would then spread in an opaque cloud, confusing the belemnite's predator.

What distinguished them from present-day squids, though, was their hard shelly internal skeleton, the most commonly preserved part being the guard. This bullet- or cigar-shaped solid calcareous structure extended into the belemnite's tail and served as a counterweight, balancing the main part of the body, including the arms and legs, located at the opposite end of the buoyancy chamber, which it also protected. The guard itself was composed of fibres of lime carbonate. As the animal grew, extra fibres were added to the guard in concentric layers like the growth rings of a tree trunk.

Belemnite guards occur in great abundance in certain areas of Europe and were well known to ancient peoples. The first written reference to the word 'belemnite' appears in the treatise *De Natura Fossilium*, published in 1546 by the 'Father of Mineralogy', Georgius Agricola. The word itself came from the Greek *belemnon*, meaning a dart. The ancient Greeks themselves called them by the name *lynkourion*, and the Romans called them *lapis lyncis*, both expressions meaning 'lynx-stone', and based on the idea that they were the excrement of wild cats. Around the shores of Kawhia Harbour, New Zealand, Maori children used to gather belemnites to play with and called them 'rokekanae', or excrement of the mullet, which they thought was in the habit of leaping out of the water and leaving belemnites behind on the shore.

In medieval times belemnites were believed to be the toe and finger nails of devils drowned in Noah's flood. Later and more plausible interpretations were that belemnites were stalactites produced underground, or thunderbolts fallen from the sky ('thunder-stones'). In the seventeenth century the Sicilian naturalist and painter Agostino Scilla concluded that belemnites must be some kind of shell formed by an unknown type of mollusc. His inference we now know to have been correct, for at the beginning of the nineteenth century the French naturalists Cuvier and Lamarck were able to prove that they were the remains of extinct mulluscs related to squids and cuttlefish. More recently, in the late nineteenth and early twentieth centuries, specimens have been found in England and Germany with the whole skeleton intact and with impressions of the soft parts, including the arms (with rows of hooklets) and ink sac, outlined in the surrounding rock.

Like present-day squids, belemnites probably preyed upon fish and crustaceans and in turn were preyed upon by larger fish. Cuts, scratches and punctures on the surface of belemnite guards have been attributed to attacks by predators, and it has been suggested that the principal enemies of belemnites were sharks, ichthyosaurs and mosasaurs.

When the belemnites died and sank to the sea bottom, their flesh decayed, and usually all that survived to become fossils in the enclosing rock were the hard guards. The total body length of the original animal, from the tail to the tip of the tentacles, was probably nine or 10 times that of the guard. The largest guard known comes from Indonesia and is 457 millimetres long — making the animal probably about 4.5 metres from the tail to the tip of the tentacles. The largest guard from New Zealand is a mere 113 millimetre specimen from Waikato Heads, probably from a 1.2 metre animal. Other New Zealand belemnite guards range down to 40 millimetres long, representing animals about 0.4 metres long. These guards are found in many parts of New Zealand, and are used as 'tags' to identify rock strata in widely separated areas — notably Waikato Heads, Kawhia Harbour, Wairarapa, Haumuri Bluff (North Canterbury), Brighton (near Dunedin) and the Hokonui Hills (Southland).

The marine reptiles

The undoubted monarchs of the Mesozoic seas were, however, the large marine reptiles. Just as the dinosaurs ruled the land, so the seas were dominated by the large swimming reptiles.

After successfully conquering the land in the Carboniferous and Permian some reptiles had staged a return to the sea in the Triassic and from these emerged three main groups — the ichthyosaurs, plesiosaurs and mosasaurs — each having contrasting appearances and each exploiting different ecological niches. In New Zealand fossils of all three groups have been found in Hawke's Bay, Marlborough, Canterbury and Otago.

The smallest of these were the 'fish-lizards' or

LEFT: *The fearsome jaw and teeth of a mosasaur of late Cretaceous age (Waipara Gorge, Canterbury).* BELOW: *Preserved mosasaur bones (Mangahouanga Stream, Hawke's Bay). Attaining lengths of 14–15 metres, mosasaurs were the most rapacious marine predators of the Mesozoic seas.* RIGHT: *Ichthyosaurs or 'fish lizards' superficially resembled the modern dolphin, and averaged about three metres in length.*

ichthyosaurs that averaged about three metres in length, although some attained an impressive 13 metres. With their fish-like bodies, large crescented tail fin, large triangular dorsal fin, and limbs flattened and fused together to form hydrofoil-shaped paddles, they resembled the modern dolphin — a mammal similarly adapted to life in the sea. Unlike the dolphin, their long pointed jaws were armed with numerous large sharp teeth, sometimes as many as 200. So armed, ichthyosaurs preyed on the many fish inhabiting the continental shelves, and apparently had a penchant for the succulent cephalopods. We know this from the stomach contents of these creatures that have been miraculously preserved. Belemnites had tiny barbed hooks on their tentacles and a hard internal skeleton. These would have resisted the digestive processes of the ichthyosaur's stomach and probably would have remained in the stomach for a while before being eventually excreted. By examining the stomach contents of one particular ichthyosaur, it has been estimated that it had dined on nearly 1,600 belemnites before it died — a staggering feast considering the creature only measured 1.5 metres in length.

The most renowned of the marine reptiles was undoubtedly the long-necked sea serpent or plesiosaur — immortalised in the popular imagination by its association with the so-called Loch Ness monster. What chiefly characterised this creature was its exceedingly long neck and small head. Incongruously, the rest of its body was small and compact, its tail rather short and stumpy. A small triangular dorsal fin ran along the middle of the back and there were four large paddle limbs for swimming. Their overall length was often of the order of 6-8 metres, although fossils of New Zealand plesiosaurs have been found with 6.5 metre-long necks and overall body lengths of 14 metres. Although their long necks made them ill-adapted for diving and strong swimming, plesiosaurs were nonetheless very agile on the surface of the water and were able to make quick turns to snap up with their numerous fine sharp teeth the shoals of fish swimming by.

The most rapacious predators of the Mesozoic seas, roaming across vast stretches of ocean and diving to great depths, were the mosasaurs — the third group of marine reptiles. These fearful monsters were the great marine lizards, closely related to the present-day monitors but attaining lengths of up to 14-15 metres. Superficially, their bodies resembled those of the plesiosaurs although they had short necks and large heads. Their jaws, often a metre or more in length, were armed with large conical teeth and their limbs were flattened and modified into stout paddles. A massive musculature pulled the limbs down and back, making them powerful swimmers, capable of pursuing swift prey to considerable depths (300-500 metres) where many belemnites, like the modern squids, may have lived. Nothing, large or small, would have escaped their attention, and one ammonite which has been studied bears the puncture marks from 16 successive bites as the mosasaur repeatedly bit across the shell trying to pull the animal out of its shell in order to swallow it.

(Continued on page 58.)

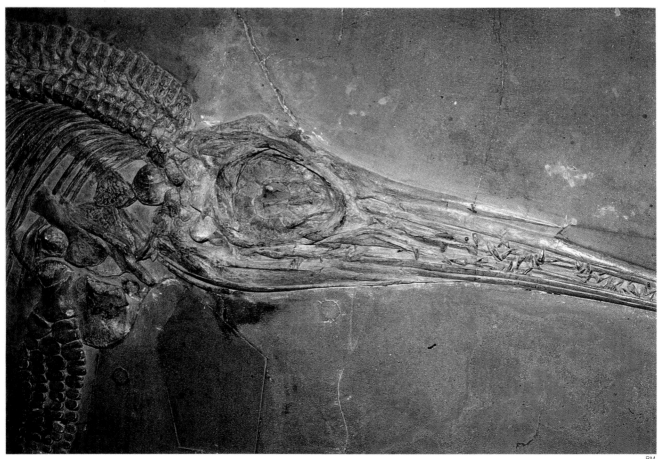

RM

Long-necked plesiosaurs, a mosasaur and a flock of
pterosaurs gather to feed on fish in this scene, set off the
coast of New Zealand in the Late Cretaceous.

The Great Die-Out

The end of the Cretaceous, 65 million years ago, saw a dramatic die-out of many of the animal and plant groups that had dominated so many Mesozoic environments. Although other periods of extinction had occurred in the course of geological time (for example, at the close of the Cambrian, Devonian, Permian and Triassic times), the magnitude and apparent suddenness of the Cretaceous extinctions has fired the imaginations of both the public and scientists. Another factor which focussed attention on Cretaceous extinctions was that dinosaurs, after completely dominating land life for some 175 million years, suddenly died out, never to be seen again.

Yet the dinosaurs were not the only living things to die out 65 million years ago. In the air the flying reptiles disappeared, but birds and flying insects appear to have been largely unaffected. On the land several groups of mammals became extinct, particularly some of those related to opossums. Other mammals, as well as small reptiles, salamanders and frogs, insects, freshwater clams and snails seem to have survived unscathed. Some changes also occurred in land plants, but not to the same extent as in the land animals. Although some flowering plants became extinct, ferns and cone-bearing trees were largely unaffected.

In the sea many inhabitants of the plankton died out, including many of the types of microscopic calcareous algae (coccoliths) and many of the microscopic single-celled animals called foraminifera. In New Zealand such foraminiferal extinctions occur in a number of sites throughout the country: in the Te Uri Stream (Dannevirke area), the Ward area and Clarence Valley (Marlborough), Waipara River and Haumuri Bluff (North Canterbury) and the Dunedin-Shag Point area (Otago).

Thinning-out or extinctions also occurred in shellfish (both bivalves and gastropods), brachiopods, bryozoa, corals, sand dollars, starfish and seas eggs, crustacea, sharks and sea turtles. However, the groups that survived, although sometimes with greatly reduced numbers, later expanded to form the nucleus of modern sea life.

In New Zealand the sheer scale of such extinctions is suggested by the abundance of marine fossils found in such localities as the Clarence Valley, Waipara River and Haumuri Bluff. There, the bones of mosasaurs and plesiosaurs are encased in concretions (large rounded mineral accumulations looking like enormous cannonballs). The fossils of bivalves, gastropods, ammonites and belemnites are also found in these areas in abundance. All these fossils disappear at the boundary of the Cretaceous period — giving a New Zealand version of the Great Die-Out.

Such was the devastating enormity of this event that it has been estimated that three-quarters of all living creatures in the world died out. Why so many died, while others were little or not affected, is one of the most baffling aspects of the 65 million-year-old mystery.

As far as we know, all these extinctions occurred worldwide simultaneously. Numerous scientists have pondered on the reasons for the massive extinctions. It has been suggested that the dinosaurs died of chronic constipation as they tried to adapt from a diet of the resinous

Many fossils date from the end-Cretaceous boundary, 65 million years ago, when global mass extinctions occurred. Euscalpellum zelandicum, which until recently was thought to be a stalked barnacle (Waipara Gorge, Canterbury).

giant ferns, clubmosses, horsetails and other plants of the Mesozoic to the more advanced and perhaps less laxative angiosperms of the Cretaceous. Then there is the idea that the dinosaur eggs, left unattended, provided easy meals for the small mammals that were then beginning to become quite numerous. Another, rather sad, suggestion is that as the climate cooled, the cold-blooded dinosaurs were all too big to find any suitable cranny in which to hibernate (smaller dinosaurs having died out earlier in the Cretaceous).

Extinctions occurred, however, in the depths of the seas, as well as on the land, and affected a great variety of plants and animals. No single explanation suffices and the extinctions were undoubtedly the result of a complex combination of circumstances.

The transition from the Mesozoic to the Cenozoic, 65 million years ago, was marked by major changes throughout the world. In many respects the Mesozoic was marked by relative calm, and the South-West Pacific was one of the few regions to experience the turmoil of mountain-building during this time. Also, because of the various groupings of the continents, a fair proportion of the world enjoyed tropical, subtropical or warm-temperate conditions. All this started to change however, as the Cretaceous drew to a close.

To judge from the records preserved in the rocks a whole host of things were happening at once, all generating major changes in the environment. In both Northern and Southern Hemispheres continents were beginning to move apart, and this led to changes in ocean basins and climates (re-routing of ocean currents, wind systems, positioning of more land close to the poles). At the same time earth movements, linked to the various continental break-ups, were occurring in many regions. These, together with changes in ocean basins, may have had far-reaching environmental consequences. Falling sea levels (resulting from either uplift of the land, or deepening of the ocean basins) may have disturbed many habitats on both land and continental shelf; rising sea levels, on the other hand, would have diminished many terrestrial habitats and forced changes onto shallow-water organisms.

As seas transgressed, nutrients from the land dwindled, plankton productivity in the seas declined and marine food chains were disturbed. Active mountain building also had the same effect — smothering the terrestrial and marine environments with coarse gravel and sand and disturbing the supply of nutrients.

Volcanic activity accompanying earth movements may have laid waste or poisoned many environments and the volcanic dust thrown up into the atmosphere may have seriously diminished the amount of the sun's energy received on earth, leading to a cooling of climate and a decrease in photosynthesis in plants.

Extra-terrestrial effects may also have had a part to play. A supernova close to the earth, or a giant solar flare, may have led to an increase in high-energy radiation, exposing organisms both on land and in the sea to the possibility of genetic damage (leading to mutations etc.). The increased radiation may also have boosted the production of nitrogen oxides (by combining nitrogen and oxygen) in the atmosphere, leading to a chemical 'smog' that would filter out the sunlight, cooling the earth and adversely affecting plant growth.

Evidence suggests also that the Mesozoic-Cenozoic boundary coincides with a major magnetic polarity reversal. If, as a consequence of the polarity change, the earth's magnetism was lost for a time and the various layers in the atmosphere that protect us from cosmic radiation (and are held in place by the magnetic field) were temporarily thinned, or lost altogether, then organisms on the earth would have been exposed to serious radiation damage.

A recent theory that has attracted a lot of attention involves an asteroid some 10-15 kilometres across colliding with the earth. This theory is based partly on the presence in various parts of the world (including Marlborough, New Zealand) of unusually high (but still minute) concentrations of platinum metals (platinum, iridium, osmium, etc.) occurring in the bands of clay deposited in layers at the boundary between the Cretaceous and Paleocene. Such metals, especially iridium, are exceedingly rare on the earth's surface but occur in high concentrations in cosmic matter from outer space. Further microscopic study of the boundary layers has also revealed similarly widespread, high concentrations of tiny droplets of glass, called spherules, formed by the congealing of molten or vapourised rock that has been splashed out from the site of some impact such as an asteroid hitting the earth.

Present in these boundary layers is also common rock quartz. When viewed under a microscope, however, many of the quartz grains are found to have an unusual structure. The grains are criss-crossed by narrow, parallel lines of glass — shock fractures caused by the grain being subjected to a sudden wave of extremely high pressure. Similar shock features have been identified in quartz grains at known meteorite impact craters and in nuclear explosions.

Yet as tantalising as all this is, until recently the crucial evidence was still pretty thin. Like the 'smoking' gun of popular detective fiction, the impact crater needed to be found before the theory could be conclusively validated.

In the 1980s geologists embarked on a worldwide hunt for such a crater and by the end of the decade the trail had been narrowed to the Caribbean. In Haiti a bed of spherules was found with droplets so large (8 mm) that they must come from a source reasonably close by. Using geological survey maps provided by a number of oil companies, the impact site was eventually pinpointed to the north-west coast of the Yucatan Peninsula in Mexico. Although by now this crater is deeply buried under younger sediments, we can tell that its diameter ranges from 180-250 kilometres — clearly one of the biggest impact structures on the earth's surface. Its sheer size makes it more than big enough to be the impact of a space body of between 10 to 20 kilometres across.

Yet how can such a comparatively small body wreak so much damage and the sort of devastation sufficient to result in the mass extinctions that occurred at the end of the Cretaceous? For this, we only have to look at the effect of major volcanic eruptions in historical times. The effects of the eruptions of the Indonesian volcanoes of Tamboro in 1815 and Krakatoa in 1883 were felt as far away as New Zealand. More recently, the eruption of Mount Pinatubo in the Philippines blocked out about 3 per cent of the heat from the sun and in New Zealand resulted in a general lowering of some 0.5 or 1.0 degrees Celsius and cool unsettled summers in 1991-92 and 1992-93.

The most dramatic recent basis for comparison was provided by the spacecraft Galileo when it recorded what happened in 1994 when fragments of the Comet Shoemaker-Levy 9 smashed into Jupiter. The largest fragment, when it hit Jupiter, produced a flash and fireball that momentarily exceeded the brightness of the entire planet. A plume of superheated gas then erupted and rose to a height of some 2000 kilometres. The most conservative estimate of the size of this fragment places it at a diameter of 3-4 kilometres and it is estimated that it hit Jupiter with an explosive energy equivalent to about 6 million megatonnes of TNT. If this comparatively small object was able to tear an earth-sized hole in Jupiter, can we reasonably doubt the catastrophic effect of a much larger strike upon our much smaller planet?

When the Yucatan asteroid crashed to earth at the end of Cretaceous, it would have thrown up a vast blanket of vapourised carbon and sulphur dioxides, intermingled with fine dust. The resulting dense haze would have filtered out enough sunlight to drop surface temperatures to near freezing levels for up to a decade. Over time, carbonic and sulphuric acids washed out of the atmosphere to produce levels of acid rain that would make today's pollution in industrialised Europe and North America seem paltry.

The actual impact would have triggered massive earthquakes, vastly bigger than the largest measured earthquake we know about. Out to sea, the collapse of enormous quantities of soft sediments from off the face of the continental slope would have generated a succession of giant tsunami waves. These radiated outwards from the impact zone and surged backwards and forwards across the ancestral Gulf of Mexico and the Caribbean. The waves reared up on to the land, clawing back into the sea anything that could be moved. Offshore, on the continental shelf, the waves scoured and stripped consolidated beds of sand and mud from the sea bed and, on retreating, dumped in their place chaotically jumbled masses of rocky blocks, gravel and course sand.

It is likely that the Yucatan asteroid was one of several impacts since smaller craters, measuring some 20-35 kilometres across and dating from the same time, have been found in Iowa and Siberia. A possible scenario would envisage the earth's surface being bombarded by a sequence of strikes, over a span of 1.5 million years, arising from the breaking up of a comet or large meteorite. Some fragments would have merely grazed the earth's atmosphere, but would have left in their wake devastating continental bush fires that would have generated a potentially lethal earth-enshrouding veil of smoke, dust and soot. Not surprisingly, quantities of soot and the remains of burnt vegetation have been found at some end-Cretaceous sites.

The scale of the extinctions is numbing, so complete the catastrophe. Many plants and animals died out on land and in the sea. Only those plants that could regenerate from buried root systems, or those with resistant long-living seeds, would have survived. Among the animals, only those small scavanging animals feeding on the dead animal and plant life would have managed to hang on until the skies cleared. Among the survivors of this Diluvian ark were the ancestral mammals. The way was now open for them, and eventually humans, to take the centre of the world's stage.

4. A southern Atlantis

After 100 million years of sustained erosion, the ancestral landmass was virtually submerged — the largest drowned continent in the world. In the sea marine life thrived, but on what land remained these were stressful times for plants and animals.

CRETACEOUS	Paleocene	Eocene	Oligocene	Miocene
65 m.y.a.	53 m.y.a.	37 m.y.a.	24 m.y.a.	

BY the beginning of the Cenozoic — the most recent of the great geological eras — the ancestral New Zealand landmass had been so worn away that much of the land was at a low level and sea was flooding in across the lowest parts of the eroded land, including Northland and the east coasts of both islands. Little if any hilly terrain remained and extensive rolling, densely forested plainlands stretched virtually the length and breadth of the land. In low-lying areas enormous swamplands had formed, clothed in luxuriant subtropical vegetation and, as time passed, thicknesses of plant material accumulated in the subsiding swamp basins. Much later, after being subjected to heat and pressure, these swamps were to produce the coalfields of north-west Nelson and the oil and gas fields of Taranaki.

It was about this time that the ancestors of New Zealand's short-tailed bat (*Mystacina tuberculata*) migrated here — our only native land mammal. (New Zealand's only other bat species, the long-tailed bat (*Chalinolobus tuberculatus*) is a relatively recent immigrant from Australia, presumably blown across the Tasman by westerly storms.) Like the tuatara, *Mystacina* is the only one of its type in the world and is the living representative of a very ancient bat lineage. Bats are believed to have evolved about 80-100 million years ago in the Cretaceous period from small tree-living shrew-like mammals. Ancestral bats spread rapidly throughout the tropical and subtropical regions and blood testing points to a South American connection for *Mystacina* in the distant past. To reach here the bat would have had to cross West Antarctica before the ice cap developed and then to cross the newly formed Southern Ocean before it became too wide and stormy — a hazardous journey for such a small animal.

In the absence of mammalian predators the migrant *Mystacina* became an adept land-dweller, flourishing in the lush Paleocene forests. Among the most terrestrial of all bats, they are astonishingly active on the forest floor, searching out leaf litter and scuttling up tree trunks and along branches with rodent-like agility.

Ancestors of three distinctive families of New Zealand land birds may also have arrived some time in the Paleocene as wind-blown immigrants across the infant Tasman Sea and Southern Ocean. These families are found nowhere else in the world, and are presumably long-standing residents. They include the New Zealand wrens (rifleman, bush wren, rock wren, Stephens Island wren), the native thrushes (piopio) and the wattlebirds (huia, saddleback and kakako). The ancestors of the kiwis may also have arrived after a flight across the widening Tasman. Not surprisingly, the only land-based animals apparently able to cross the infant Tasman Sea and Southern Ocean as they were opening were those endowed with the power of flight: bats and birds. Other land mammal groups, unable to fly, were excluded. From the drowning of Atlantis, Island New Zealand had formed.

On the move again

During the Paleocene the global rifting movements begun during the late Cretaceous continued to break up Gondwana with the effect that New Zealand was now being shunted northwards away from the South Pole and its southern land links so that in the Paleocene it occupied a more temperate latitude of 50–45°S, compared with 65–66°S latitude in the late Cretaceous. This northerly drift, and the continued creation of new sea floor to the south of New Zealand, eventually broke the southern shallow-water marine links between New Zealand, Australia, West Antarctica and South America. At the same time, sea-floor spreading in the Tasman Sea, which had started in late Cretaceous times 80 million years ago, continued into the early Paleocene and only drew to a close 60 million years ago when the Tasman reached its present width of 1,850 kilometres.

As the creation of new sea floor ended in the Tasman, the focus of sea-floor spreading shifted to the south-west, to the area between Australia and Antarctica. Although some splitting and rifting had been going on for some 40 million years previously, a wedge of new ocean floor now began to appear between these two continents some 55 million years ago, at the close of the Paleocene. As Australia and Antarctica moved apart, the zone of actively spreading sea floor between them linked up with that already in existence south of New Zealand. Australia and New Zealand thus began to move northwards together until by the late Eocene (37 million years ago) New Zealand's geographic position was 45–40°S latitude, compared with 50–45°S in the Paleocene.

The parting of the ways

At about the same time, in the late Eocene, the opening of the South Fiji Basin to the north of New Zealand broke the long-standing links between New Zealand and New

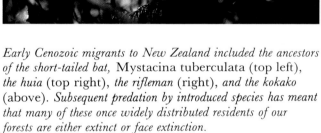

Early Cenozoic migrants to New Zealand included the ancestors of the short-tailed bat, Mystacina tuberculata *(top left), the huia (top right), the rifleman (right), and the kokako (above). Subsequent predation by introduced species has meant that many of these once widely distributed residents of our forests are either extinct or face extinction.*

Caledonia. The intensity and scale of these tearing and rifting movements was so violent that during the Oligocene (37–25 million years ago) a vast piece of ancient oceanic crust was thrust up over New Caledonia and in northern New Zealand, north of Auckland, entire chunks of country were turned upside down, thrust over each other and jumbled around in a chaotic mess.

From almost the beginning of their geological histories New Zealand and New Caledonia had shared geological events and were probably parts of the same ancestral landmass. New Caledonia had also shared in New Zealand's primitive terrestrial flora and fauna and although, as in New Zealand, 'thinning out' has occurred, geographic isolation has ensured that many interesting relics remain. Now these sea floor movements had rifted New Zealand and New Caledonia apart, and from here onwards both countries went their separate ways.

It is uncanny to go some 1,300 kilometres across the sea to New Caledonia and there see a country with so many faunal and floral similarities to New Zealand — a country with a primitive flightless bird as a national symbol (the cagou, *Rhynochetos*), and a forest with so many New Zealand types (treeferns, podocarps, *Nothofagus*). Like New Zealand, New Caledonia lacks land snakes and marsupials, and its only mammal is a native bat that presumably winged its way across the infant Tasman early in the Cenozoic. However, unlike New Zealand, it lacks indigenous amphibians, primarily freshwater fish and freshwater mussels, even as fossils. Although it lacks spectacular primitive animals such as New Zealand's tuatara and native frog, New Caledonia more than makes up for it in the plant kingdom. It teems with primitive plants, and probably no richer, nor more peculiar, archaic and endemic relics of plant life can be found elsewhere in the world compressed into such a small area — one-seventh the size of the North Island.

Antarctica: the frozen continent

The deep-sea basins that had formed between New Zealand and New Caledonia were part of general rifting movements then underway throughout the southern oceans. We must now return to the wedge of new sea floor that since the close of the Paleocene had been growing between Australia and Antarctica. These two continents, as if obeying the fundamental principle of Newtonian physics, were being pushed apart in opposite directions so that while Australia moved north, Antarctica moved equally further south. The Antarctic continent had begun to exert an influence at the southern Pacific whose profound consequences are still controlling the development of many of today's environments.

As Antarctica moved south, and as the cold polar marine currents began to flow around the now ocean-encircled continent, ice fields formed on the mountain tops and fingers of glaciers began to reach down the valleys. For the first time since the Permian a landmass of continental proportions was positioned on the South Pole.

What unfolds is the poignant tale of how a once-verdant continent, covered in a profuse and diverse ecology, was gradually overwhelmed by ice and snow. Much of what we know is recounted from core samples of sea-floor sediment that accumulated around Antarctica over the last 60 million years. The samples were obtained as part of an internationally supported research effort, the Ocean Drilling Project — accomplished in often difficult conditions in stormy seas five kilometres deep, and in the presence of huge menacing icebergs that had to be lassoed and towed out of the way by support ships.

Study of the core samples shows that the Antarctica of the past did not function as a single climatic unit as it does today, but rather that East and West Antarctica, separated by one of the world's great mountain systems, the Trans-Antarctic Mountains, had somewhat different climatic histories.

Initially, some 60 million years ago, at a time when marsupials were migrating from western Antarctica to Australia, both East and West Antarctica had a warm,

humid climate, but then over the next 20 million years, as Antarctica moved southwards, the climate gradually changed to become temperate.

The presence of extensive areas of rugged high country close to the pole generated unsettled stormy conditions and formed a focal point for the accumulation of snow and ice. The valleys and depressions of the high country also provided gathering grounds in which snow became compacted into hard glacier ice. Once formed, the glacier ice flowed outwards, under the influence of gravity, covering the surrounding lands. Judging from core samples, ice first started to lie on the Antarctic mountain tops in the early Eocene, about 53-50 million years ago.

By late Eocene (40–37 million years ago), a major cooling phase had occurred and glacier ice had reached the East Antarctic coast. The ice, fed from icefields inland, pushed out from the coastline and the first sea ice began to form. The presence of minute grains of fossil pollen

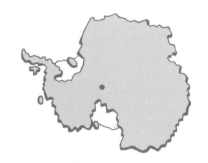

and spores in sediment indicates that up to about 30 million years ago both East and West Antarctica were still extensively clothed with reasonably continuous beech forest and that the climate was probably similar to that of south-west Westland today. In East Antarctica a New Zealand drilling project obtained from McMurdo Sound a well-preserved beech leaf from 30 million-year-old mudstones lying between glacial beds. The glaciation present then was still largely confined to the high country with only a few of the larger glaciers sending tongues of ice down some of the main valleys.

Initially, the Antarctic beech forests could probably have lived alongside the glaciers and ice fields, as they do today in Patagonia and southern New Zealand, but

eventually chilling resulted in the massive expansion of ice and the retreat of plant and animal life. This began in East Antarctica about 33 million years ago. In West Antarctica the build-up of ice was a lot slower and 20 million years ago freshwater lakes — rather than ice and snow — were still present in the Antarctic Peninsula. On the coast thick growths of kelp still fringed the shore. Glacial debris only first appears in the sediments laid down on the floor of the Weddell Sea some 15 million years ago. At first the glacial debris was spasmodic, but then towards eight million years ago, it became more constant, indicating the steady build-up of the main West Antarctic ice sheet. Even then there were periods when the ice melted, feeding rivers that deposited sand and

RIGHT: *Snow drifts shaped by wind on the beach at Cape Evans, Ross Island, Antarctica.*
BELOW: *Looking south from Lewis Bay to Mt Terror (3262 metres), Ross Island, Antarctica.*

RM

'Goblin' or 'elf' forest in the Southern Alps. The extinction of forest life in Antarctica probably went through a similar sequence of events to that experienced by sub-alpine flora today.

gravel on the continental shelf. Periodically these accumulations cascaded down the sea floor slope forming characteristic submarine landslides. These sand and gravel slide deposits vanish after about 4.8 million years ago; coastal fossils, particularly of minute plankton requiring sunlit waters, also disappear about this time. West Antarctica had joined East Antarctica in being permanently covered with ice. The Big Freeze had begun in earnest.

With nowhere to retreat, forest life on the Antarctic continent had become extinct, its chorus of forest bird song perpetually stilled. Just how this would have happened can be graphically illustrated by the changes in vegetation observed as one travels south towards Tierra del Fuego at the southernmost tip of South America. At first the forest vegetation is virtually identical to that of any beech forest in southern New Zealand — almost uncannily so. But then, getting further and further south, the once proud beech trees become thinned out and stunted until they are reduced to sparse groups of low spindly shrub-like plants, providing a skimpy coverage to the ground. Eventually it becomes too frigid for even these pathetic remnants — mere apologies for trees — and the landscape becomes largely a barren waste, dotted with patches of mosses, lichens and alpine grasses and herbs, culminating in terrain perpetually capped by snow and ice.

The same sequence of changing vegetation can be observed on our own mountainsides. The plant life living there responds to the increasing cold by progressively phasing out less tolerant types and introducing in their place types with a greater tolerance to chilling climates. A series of life zones can be observed, each one typified by distinctive plant types. Although the zones can be distinguished, following each other in a vertical sequence, often their boundaries are blurred by irregular terrain or differences in soil, rainfall and exposure to sun and wind.

In the lowlands of much of New Zealand podocarp forest predominates and may even be found on many of the lower North Island mountains. Elsewhere, especially in the South Island and some North Island areas south of Hamilton, podocarps are soon left behind in the valleys and the mountainsides are almost exclusively the domain of *Nothofagus*, the southern beech. These continue to populate the slopes, becoming progressively smaller and more thinly spaced on the higher slopes. As the amount of frost-free growing time decreases so the dense stands of trees dwindle and thin out until the treeline is reached. There trees are not only stunted by the cold but are also deformed by the bitingly cold and fierce winds. Often at the treeline the forest will dwindle into ragged lines and patches of dwarfed wind-bent tangles of ground-hugging gnarled trees and shrub — called 'goblin' or 'elfin' forest by climbers. These goblin forests clinging to the slopes represent the very last stand of the trees against the cold and chilling winds. Above the treeline even the most hardy species fail to survive and give way to shrubs, lichens, mosses and eventually to barren wastes. This is the domain of snow and ice.

So the ecology of Antarctica went through a similar sequence of events but spaced out over a length of time spanning millions of years. Certainly all indications are that by Pliocene times at the latest, 5 million years ago, Antarctica had virtually been submerged under a thick ice cap, signalling the end of forest life on the frozen continent.

The Southern Ocean

The expansion of ice on Antarctica had an obvious cooling effect on the waters of the Southern Hemisphere. This was also accompanied by changes in the patterns of oceanic currents within the surrounding seas — changes that were to enhance the cooling already occurring on Antarctica and transport cool Antarctic water into many southern regions. Such changes could only take place, however, after the southern lands had separated from Antarctica, leaving the southern oceans clear of barriers and able to circulate freely.

Although open sea had first appeared around Antarctica in the late Cretaceous (80 million years ago), when Africa and New Zealand began to pull away, followed by South America (70–65 million years ago), it was not until late Paleocene times (55 million years ago) that Australia and Antarctica began to separate — the last remaining landmasses to drift apart. At first, as Australia and Antarctica pulled apart, the gap between the two continents had been filled by a shallow sea stirred by weak ocean currents. This shallow sea with its limited circulation had continued to exist to almost the end of the Eocene (40–37 million years ago) when marine life was still able to move from the south-east Indian Ocean across the South Tasman Rise and into the south-east Pacific Ocean. The final separation of Gondwana occurred during middle and late Oligocene time (34–24 million years ago) when Tasmania, and more critically its submarine continuation as the South Tasman Rise, had moved clear of the northern tip of Antarctica's Victoria Land. A distinctively southern oceanic circum-Antarctic current system was now able to develop.

The stirring of the Southern Ocean by the infant circum-Antarctic current system spread cool water, derived from the Antarctic glaciers, northwards into surrounding regions and many southern areas began to feel the effects of influxes of cool Antarctic water during late Eocene and Oligocene times. In New Zealand subtropical environments were gradually replaced in late Eocene and Oligocene times by more temperate environments as sea water temperatures dropped to those now found around the coasts of the Campbell and Auckland Islands.

An important consequence of the onset of Antarctic glaciation was an expansion of the life in the Southern Ocean. As the Antarctic glaciers became more extensive they began to work on the enormous range of rock materials that are present on a continent the size of Antarctica. Scouring, shattering and the general disintegration of rock by the effects of glacial erosion produced vast quantities of fine mineral powder called 'rock flour' that eventually found its way into the surrounding oceans, either from glaciers directly entering the sea or from rivers draining the ice-covered inland areas. The nutrient-rich Southern Ocean now became the setting for a massive expansion of planktonic populations. The microscopic organisms that make up the plankton in the seas depend on the supply of nutrients and the amount of sunlight penetrating the water for their survival. Tiny single-celled floating plants called phytoplankton float freely in the upper layers of the sea where there is sufficient light for them to convert through photosynthesis nutrient minerals into plant tissues. These phytoplankton comprise the oceans' pastures, as it were, and are grazed upon by minute animals called zooplankton. Together the phyto- and zooplankton form the basis for innumerable complex and often interwoven food chains in the seas. These food chains grow with animals of increasing size and sophistication consuming and in turn being consumed. Some of the larger animals feed directly on the larger forms of zooplankton. Planktonic shrimps (euphausids or 'krill') are consumed in enormous quantities by whales. Krill are also eaten by such fish as trevally, mackerel, and anchovies. The smaller of these fish in turn become the food of larger fish-eating predators such as sharks, barracouta, John Dory, tuna and marlin.

These food chains form a pyramid of life — with those animals near the base being very small and enormously abundant and those at the apex large but

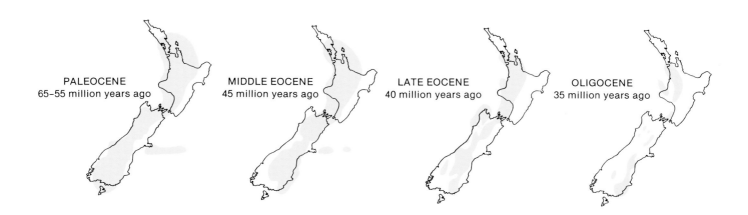

PALEOCENE
65–55 million years ago

MIDDLE EOCENE
45 million years ago

LATE EOCENE
40 million years ago

OLIGOCENE
35 million years ago

The cetaceans evolved from small wolf-like land mammals, known as *creodonts*, that 50 million years ago made the transition from land to the sea. (A) *archaeocete*, the primitive ancestral whale; (B) Arnoux's beaked whale; (C) sperm whale.

comparatively few in number. Not surprisingly, the rapid expansion of planktonic life in the Southern Ocean during the late Paleocene saw a corresponding expansion in the populations of other marine animals, and from the early Eocene the New Zealand region played a leading role in the development of groups such as Cetacea (whales, dolphins and porpoises) and penguins.

The evolution of the cetaceans provides one of the most striking examples of an animal group taking advantage of an environmental opportunity and then adapting to that environment. The extinction of the large marine reptiles at the end of the Cretaceous left empty the niches they had formerly occupied. These were now filled by ocean-going mammals, of which one of the first groups to appear was the cetaceans. The earliest cetacean fossils occur in the early Eocene of Pakistan and their characteristics suggest that they were ungulate (hoofed) animals which made a gradual change from land into the sea, spending more and more time feeding in the plankton-rich shallow waters of the eastern Tethys Ocean. Although these ancestral cetaceans had not fully adapted to a marine existence — they lacked modifications for hearing under water, for example — by early Oligocene times ancestors of toothed whales, dolphins and porpoises (odontoceti) and baleen whales (mysticeti) had appeared in New Zealand waters.

Another group of animals to exploit the bountiful Southern Ocean at this time were the shorebirds. In the Cretaceous the descendants of *Archaeopteryx* had begun to occupy a number of important ecological niches, particularly around the shorelines of lakes and seas. Then in the late Cretaceous, about 70 million years ago, fish-eating cormorants and waders evolved in the USA. Shore-birds continued to be dominant in the Paleocene and

Eocene and types similar to flamingos, cranes and rails were diverse although the song birds (Passeriformes), by far the most diverse birds of today, hadn't yet appeared.

Perhaps the most spectacular shorebirds to evolve during the Eocene were the 'false-toothed' birds or pseudodontorns whose fossils have been found in many localities throughout the world. In New Zealand the fossil of one species, *Neodontornis*, has been found in Pliocene rocks at Motunau, North Canterbury, while that of another species, *Pelagornis*, has been found in Miocene rocks in North Canterbury, and is identical to a specimen found in Miocene rocks in France. These birds were rather like enormous gannets and could swallow kahawai-sized fish by hinging their lower jaw. All of the false-toothed birds had bony tooth-like projections along the sides of the bill. Although such 'teeth' looked like true reptilian teeth, they were simply bony continuations of the jawbone and lacked the enamel and dentine charac-teristics of real teeth.

Although we don't know the exact sequence of events, a group of ancestral shorebirds living in the southern oceans became adapted for a more fully marine life, and from these penguins evolved. The fossil occurrences of penguins fall within their modern geographic range. Today penguins are found in southern New Zealand, southern Australia, the sub-Antarctic and Antarctic islands, Antarctica, Argentina, Chile and southern South Africa, but the largest concentrations and greatest numbers of species occur in cold-temperate, sub-Antarctic and Antarctic seas.

The oldest known fossil penguin is a skeleton dating from the early Eocene, 50 million years ago, and was found in north Canterbury in 1986. The preserved skeleton consists of the wing, leg and head of a bird which stood some 60 centimetres high, and from its bone structure we have been able to determine that it had only recently evolved from a flying bird ancestor. Even today penguins 'fly' rather than 'swim' in the water. In the radical change from flying in a light medium (air) to flying in a dense medium (sea water), penguins have retained large flying muscles in their chest and all the bones of a flying wing — their flippers are merely flying wings modified for flight in water rather than air.

Diving petrels, like penguins, also 'fly' underwater but are capable of aerial flight as well. Within modern families of diving birds there is a definite weight limit, probably about one kilogram, beyond which excessive wing loading makes flying difficult. And yet, a body size larger than one kilogram facilitates sustained diving and allows birds wider scope in hunting. Everything points to the possibility that sometime in the Eocene penguins were petrel-like diving birds that lost the power of flight when they opted for underwater expertise. Like the Cetacea, they had abandoned one environment when the opportunities to exploit another more successfully became apparent.

Having made the transition to water, penguins flourished and by the late Eocene had reached their maximum development. The largest known fossil penguin, rejoicing in the name *Pachydyptes ponderosus*, dated from this time and was found at Oamaru and described in 1930. Whereas modern emperor penguins weigh some 30 kilograms and have a standing height of about one metre, the Oamaru giant probably weighed a massive 100 kilograms and stood 1.62 metres — about the height of the average person.

The weathered stump

The penguins that struggled ashore on to the New Zealand coastline during the late Eocene would have encountered a vastly changed land from the one those earlier migrants, the *Mystacina* bats, had encountered 25 million years before. Now isolated and separated from all continental links New Zealand had since Paleocene times undergone still further erosion and general wearing-down until the ancestral landmass was virtually submerged, forming an enormous area of relatively shallow water — the largest drowned continent of the world. Standing plateau-like above the surrounding oceanic depths, it lay directly in the path of the newly developing circum-Antarctic oceanic currents. Nutrient-rich water derived from Antarctica was able to spread out across a huge platform of temperate shallow water and because the little land that was present was so worn down as to be insignificant as a source of sediment the sea waters were probably quite clear, allowing good light penetration and maximum photosynthesis in the plankton. In short, everything favoured the substantial expansion of plankton life and large populations of other marine animals developed, either living off the plankton or preying on plankton feeders.

By contrast, the rather scrappy pieces of land that poked up above these extensive shallow shelf seas were probably not the most hospitable places for land creatures. The fragments of land had been worn down virtually to sea level by almost 100 million years of relentless erosion, reducing the topography to that of a gently rolling plain or peneplain.

Towards the end of Eocene times sea flooded in over

RIGHT: *King penguins and chicks (*Aptenodytes patagonicus), Macquarie Island. BELOW: *The yellow-eyed penguin (*Megadyptes antipodus) *is of a genus and species found nowhere else but in the southern oceans of New Zealand, and is thought to be a remnant species of ancient penguin.*

JOHN WARHAM

JOHN WARHAM

the extensive coastal swamps, smothering them in a layer of sand and silt — the first stage in the formation of coal. Now buried, the swamp material was sealed off from the air, its decay checked. Gradually the cellulose in the soft tissues of the plants broke down to form methane, water and carbon dioxide, leaving a peat-enriched carbonaceous woody material. As more and more silt was dumped on the swamps and the peat beds previously laid down were pushed down to successively greater depths, so the increased pressure and temperature squeezed out the water and oxygen, boosting the overall carbon content. First lignite or brown coal was formed, then bituminous coal — the sort now mined from the Greymouth district.

The original swamps, particularly those in southern Taranaki and western Cook Strait, also had other constituents apart from woody material. Many plants have varying amounts of vegetable oils and waxes in their stems and leaves and if the swamp was very wet, and especially if it was periodically invaded by the sea, numerous algae, also rich in such oils and waxes, may have flourished. These algae, on dying, became incorporated in the swamp deposits, and were eventually buried under thousands of metres of silt. Subjected to the same heat and pressure that had formed the coal, the swampy material was instead converted to methane gas that became trapped in the dome-like folds of the porous rock. Today the Maui and the smaller Kapuni fields of southern Taranaki are primarily gas fields although a light grade of oil condenses from the gas as it is drawn off from the wells.

By Oligocene times, 35 million years ago, the slow withering of New Zealand had reached its climax when virtually the entire land was worn down to a very low level. Some two-thirds of the area of modern New Zealand was now covered by sea and the remaining remnants of land consisted of an elongated, narrow-gutted archipelago and a few scattered islands. Deep seas covered the entire eastern flank of New Zealand from East Cape to South-land, and extended at least as far as National Park in the North Island. Most of the South Island was virtually under water and a deep marine trough occupied the Waiau-Hollyford region. Except for the eroded stumps of land in central and northern North Island and in inland Marlborough, south Canterbury, Otago and Fiordland, the only land poking up out of the sea was small chains of volcanic islands in inland Canterbury and Marl-borough, and at East Cape and Oamaru.

On land, these must have been very stressful times for the plants and animals. The wearing-down of the land had markedly reduced the diversity of the landscape and the number and availability of environmental niches. Although plainland, flood plain, swampland and estuarine environments were very much in evidence it is unlikely that there was anything higher than low rolling hills.

Some of the land animals and plants may have responded to these environmental challenges by evolving new varieties, better equipped to cope with the changed environmental circumstances. Other species, isolated on islands and unable to crossbreed, developed separate geographic races. It is likely that some of the patterns of geographic distribution that can be seen today in various species of our large native snails date back to these

ANDRIS APSE LTD

times when populations became isolated on different islands and evolved into species that even today still retain their separate identities. Similarly, the evolution of the moas into their various groupings (sub-families, genera and species) may have begun during the Oligocene as a response to the geographic isolation.

Nonetheless it is likely that Oligocene times presented very real difficulties for the survival of many land animals and plants. The problems of marine transgression were also being compounded by an insidious chemical process attacking the soil and rocks, rotting them from within. This process we call 'leaching' — a complex chemical interaction that bleeds the soils of their essential nutrients. These chemical leaching agents start with oxides of carbon, nitrogen and sulphur in the atmosphere, that when dissolved in rainwater form weak acidic solutions. The rainwater, on reaching the ground, mixes with a variety of organic acids — usually humic and tannic acids — given off by decomposed plant litter; these chemicals now percolate through the soil, stripping it of various minerals. If the leaching is sustained over long periods, all the elements essential for plant nutrition are removed from the soils and rocks, leaving behind the more insoluble and infertile clays and sands. Sometimes even the clay minerals are broken down into flaky particles and washed away, leaving an almost pure deposit of quartz sand that because of its stable atomic structure is chemically inert and highly resistant to erosion.

It is believed that our scraps of Oligocene land may have ended up like this — mantled with thick and pervasive blankets of impoverished soils and deeply weathered rocks. Although leaching is still a problem in some of today's soils — notably those in the gumland areas of Northland — it is worth reflecting that these soils have only had some 10,000 years of leaching whereas those of the Oligocene had almost 100 million years!

The impact of such weathering, sustained over such a long period, must have been devastating — entire species of animals and plants extinguished, never to thrive again. It defies the imagination and, indeed, when we look around for a modern equivalent of what the Oligocene land may have looked like we are hard pressed. Although the bleak heartlands of Australia and South Africa may be topographically similar, they are found in tropical, not temperate, climates. The fact is that all of the lands of the world have been affected by the enormous traumas of the Pleistocene (Ice Age) period during which dramatic climatic changes, fluctuating sea levels and earth movements all had a rejuvenating effect, however small, on the landscapes. Today, we simply can't point to some part of the world and say this is what New Zealand was like 35 million years ago.

A final impression remains. From the rolling sub-tropical forests and swamplands of the Paleocene, with their myriad animal life fossicking on the forest floor or else nesting in the canopy above, New Zealand had within the short space of 30 million years been reduced to a mere rump. On this exhausted rocky stump, this island prison, only the hardiest of plants and animals lingered on in the most stressful and difficult conditions. One thing is certain: if the weathering had continued virtually nothing would have been left.

The coastal dunes and lagoons of the Chatham
Islands, the most easterly remnant of the ancestral
New Zealand landmass. By Oligocene times New
Zealand had been reduced to a narrow-gutted
archipelago and a few scattered islands. INSET:
Kahikatea swamp forest, Westland.

5. A new land

New Zealand has never been far from a plate convergence and during Miocene times it found itself astride a zone of subduction, culminating in a new land being uplifted.

Oligocene	Miocene	Pliocene	Pleistocene
24 m.y.a.		5 m.y.a.	2 m.y.a.

AFTER nearly 100 million years of slow withering, the islands of New Zealand now became the scene of restless activity and during Miocene times, between 25 and five million years ago, patterns of folds, welts and troughs developed under the influence of earth movements as segments of land moved up and down as a series of short branching folds. Large parts of New Zealand resembled an ever-changing archipelago and a chain of active andesite volcanic islands extended from Auckland to Hokianga. It almost seems as though a kind of writhing of this part of the Pacific margin went on over most of the later Cenozoic.

As it was, New Zealand found itself involved in a major re-arrangement of the huge crustal plates which make up the surface of the south-west Pacific region. It will be recalled that after the Tasman Sea had opened up 80–60 million years ago, the focus of active sea-floor spreading had shifted to between Australia and Antarctica. From about 55 million years onwards new ocean had started to form south of Australia. This switch in sea-floor spreading from the Tasman Sea to south of Australia had rotated the New Zealand block counter-clockwise, pushing part of the floor of the Tasman Sea under the edge of eastern Australia, thrusting up the Great Dividing Range and forcing many of the rivers to drain westwards, where the Murray-Darling river system was formed. The entire eastern coast of New South Wales and Victoria was uplifted and the fractures formed during such buckling formed conduits for volcanoes such as seen in the Warrumbungle Ranges and at Robertson in New South Wales.

As Australia moved progressively northwards the continued rotation of New Zealand developed a crack in the Pacific Plate which progressively extended along what is now the Macquarie Ridge and into southern New Zealand, eventually to traverse the entire country as the Alpine Fault and its northern branches. By about 23 million years ago New Zealand found itself straddling the boundary between what are now recognised as the Indian-Australian and Pacific Plates. As the two plates jostled one another, a vast array of troughs and welts developed. The land had begun to stir.

At the same time, sea-floor spreading in the South China Sea was rotating Malaysia, Indonesia and the Philippine Islands in a southwards direction, gradually closing the gap between Indonesia and Papua New Guinea which until comparatively recent times was joined to Australia. The closer proximity of the Indo-Pacific landmasses to each other now meant that an increasing number of oceanic currents of tropical origin were able to reach the east Australian and New Zealand coasts, bringing with them a great variety of tropical organisms capable of floating or swimming across open ocean. This southward spread of tropical organisms was also helped by a general improvement in worldwide climate.

This progressive narrowing of the oceanic gap between Papua New Guinea and Indonesia is reflected in the animals able to bridge the gap at various times. In the Paleocene birds and bats had migrated from South-East Asia to Australia, and eventually on to New Zealand and New Caledonia. By the Miocene the intervening gap had so narrowed, and had probably been at least partially bridged by volcanic archipelagoes, that land snakes were able to move into Papua New Guinea and eventually into Australia. However, by this time ancestral New Zealand and New Caledonia had been isolated for some 35-40 million years from the remainder of Eastern Gondwana so that snakes were unable to reach either New Zealand or New Caledonia.

Thus, from early Miocene times tropical seas lapped the shores of New Zealand and the sea water temperatures were 5-7°C warmer than those today. Enhanced by the warmer climate and the tropical currents, a new ecology now thrived. That most exotic of tropical marine faunas, reef-building coral, lived around Northland and Auckland coasts and extended as far south as East Cape. Vast mangrove swamps created new estuarine environments. And on the barren land, from seeds carried by ocean currents, palms flourished as far south as Otago and Southland — the remnants of one such subtropical beach are preserved at Bluff Hill, Southland. The cabbage tree (*Cordyline*) became established, and from Northland to Hawke's Bay coconut groves existed.

The circum-Antarctic current

The early Miocene marked the high point of Tertiary climate — a time when tropical vegetation extended to latitudes now the preserve of temperate climates. Thereafter a period of cooling ensued as ice built up in Antarctica and from the middle and late Miocene times (15–5 million years ago) many of the tropical organisms that had previously migrated to New Zealand gradually disappeared, although sea-water temperatures around the coasts were still warmer than those of today.

As the Antarctic ice sheets grew in size and southern

climates cooled, the geography of the Southern Hemisphere began to resemble that of today. The influence of the circum-Antarctic current system on the seas surrounding Antarctica, first felt in the late Oligocene, now became greatly enhanced by the progressively widening gaps between Antarctica, South America and Australia. This allowed increasing quantities of water to be included in the current movements. As the current expanded, some tropical or subtropical marine animals, moving southwards in currents flowing from the Indo-Pacific region, were able to link up with the circum-Antarctic current and by this means became widely distributed around southern as well as tropical lands. To use but one example: our New Zealand echinoderms (starfish, brittle stars, sea eggs etc.) may have travelled southwards from the Egyptian-Indian area in Oligocene times, 30 million years ago, spread throughout Australasia and then circled the Southern Hemisphere at least once, evolving as they went, and eventually arriving back in New Zealand where they started, but from the other direction (i.e. from the west) and as different forms.

By the middle Miocene, however, major differences began to exist between the temperatures of the polar and tropical waters. These were expressed not as a continuous graduation from pole to tropics but rather as a series of belts of oceanic waters, separated by boundary zones or 'convergences' (Antarctic Convergence, Subtropical Convergence). Although these belts have largely retained their identity from Miocene through to the present day, their position with respect to latitude has fluctuated in response to episodes of global warming and cooling.

Today the circum-Antarctic current circles clockwise around Antarctica, passing just to the south of Australia and New Zealand. Unimpeded by any landmasses, it is the only oceanic current that makes major contributions to all the world's major oceans (except the Arctic Ocean). Its plankton-laden waters feed the Southern Hemisphere fisheries and it exerts a significant effect on oceanic circulation and everything that derives from this: meteorology, climate, animal and plant distributions, etc.

West Wind Drift

Once the circum-Antarctic current got into its stride, and as the Antarctic continent continued to cool, an Antarctic-centred weather pattern emerged which has continued to have a decisive influence on the Southern Hemisphere. Of the associated meteorological phenomena, the most notable is the West Wind Drift — the prevailing westerly winds that encircle the globe at latitudes between 40°S and 60°S. These we have evocatively named the 'Roaring Forties', 'Furious Fifties', and 'Screaming Sixties' — winds so powerful and so constant that they can drive surface water along at rates matching the deeper flowing circum-Antarctic current.

The combined action of wind and current must have been highly effective because once established it transported many animals and plants across the Southern Ocean and from the Miocene onwards New Zealand began to gain many new southern colonists. These, however, differed markedly from those of the Mesozoic. The southern plants and animals of the Mesozoic had travelled across and around the then closely connected southern lands and were all of types that needed either continuous land or closely adjoining islands to migrate. Even the marine creatures had needed shallow water. The

During Oligocene and early Miocene times many tropical organisms, swept by warm oceanic currents, migrated to New Zealand. These included: (below) Platyhelia distans, colonial coral from Cavendish, Canterbury; (right) Brochopleurus stellatus, sea eggs from Tarakohe, Nelson; and (far right) the nikau, our only surviving palm and the world's most southerly palm.

riders of the West Wind Drift, on the other hand, were all of types capable of crossing major stretches of ocean as eggs, larvae or adults. As the distribution of land and sea in the Southern Hemisphere from Miocene times onward was virtually as it is now, it is evident that these organisms were capable of surviving long distances over large oceanic gaps.

To return to our example of the echinoderms. The eggs of a number of echinoderms hatch out to produce a larva that is free-swimming and contains substantial quantities of yolk. This vitellaria or 'yolk-larva' has a simple cylindrical or barrel-shaped body, without arms or other projections, that is nevertheless encircled by rings of hair-like threads that beat rhythmically and so propel the vitellaria through the water. As well, the yolk supply in the vitellaria's body enables it to swim for a considerable time before exhausting its food supply and, although the time varies, some vitellariae can stay swimming in the upper layers of the sea for as long as eight weeks. If this does not sound very long, it is still long enough for the larva to travel many thousands of kilometres, pushed along by the West Wind Drift.

Another way the echinoderms get around is for the adults to 'hitch a ride' on masses of bull kelp and similar large seaweeds. Kelp and other brown seaweeds have grape-shaped, air-filled flotation structures attached to their stems and their tissues, too, are spongy and air-filled. If they are ripped free by storms they are capable of drifting for considerable distances — for example, some have drifted between Kerguelen Island and Australia, a distance of some 6,000 kilometres.

Like bull kelp, many plants with coastal habitats have buoyant fruits or seeds that can drift across the ocean, swept by currents. It is believed that plants such as the kowhai (*Sophora*) and those of the *Hebe* family migrated between New Zealand, southern Chile and Gough Island in this way.

The high winds of the 'Roaring Forties' may, in their own right, also distribute plants and animals. Many plants have light seeds or spores or plumed seeds that float freely and can be carried hundreds of kilometres by prevailing winds, eventually to drop to the earth and, if conditions are favourable, establish new colonies. In the same way, some insects use the wind to expand their distribution and will devise extraordinary means to assist them in their flight. Some spiders, for example, create web parachutes from which they are suspended like tiny balloonists, floating gamely across vast distances.

By so using the prevailing westerly winds many Australian plants and animals migrated to New Zealand from Miocene times onwards. Some, having reached New Zealand, used it as a stepping stone and continued to ride the West Wind Drift to the Chathams, Easter Island, South America and beyond.

Others arrived in New Zealand and established themselves, only to be wiped out by the frigid climates of the Ice Age. Unlike Australia, New Zealand has no retreat route northwards into tropical areas along which warmth-loving plants and animals could move to escape the rigours of the glacial climate. Thus typical Australian plants such as *Eucalyptus* (blue gum), *Casuarina* (she-oak) and *Acacia* (wattle), to judge from the excellence of their fossil record, were formerly well established in New Zealand but died out during the Ice Age.

Other immigrants arrived in New Zealand but for various reasons did not establish breeding populations.

Successful late Miocene migrants, carried by the newly developed West Wind Drift included (above) *kowhai,* Sophora microphylla, (above right) Hebe decumbens, (right) H. macrocarpa *var.* latisepala, *and* (far right) *the takahe.*

This point was brought home to zoologists during the drilling offshore from Taranaki that preceded development of the Maui gas field. During this time entomologists operating insect traps on the drilling platforms were amazed at the numbers of Australian moths and butterflies that arrived as exhausted stragglers in the wake of trans-Tasman gales. Of these only a fraction have managed to establish themselves on the New Zealand mainland.

Of the successful natural colonisers, the plants *Epilobium, Celmisia* and *Veronica* are notable examples — but equally notable absentees (until introduced artificially) were the wattles (*Acacia*) and the blue gums (*Eucalyptus*), each with over 500 species in Australia, and *Hakea* and *Grevillea*, each with over 100 species. Among the insects, blue moon butterflies and various Australian moths regularly arrive on New Zealand's west coasts. The monarch butterfly is another Australian immigrant.

Undoubtedly the most successful riders of the west wind were the birds, and the late Cenozoic saw the arrival of many land birds of Australian origin, travelling via storm-generated westerly gales. As a result, the modern New Zealand bird fauna has a strong Australian aspect. Notable exceptions are the moa and kiwi dating back to late Jurassic and early Cretaceous times when southern land links were evident. Also endemic are the families of New Zealand wrens, thrushes and wattlebirds, probably introduced as wind-assisted migrants in early Cenozoic times, before distances became too great across the widening oceans around New Zealand.

The continuing influx of storm-blown Australian land birds into New Zealand throughout late Cenozoic times has given rise to examples of multiple colonisation.

The takahe, for example, is derived from a possible Miocene-Pliocene migration across the Tasman and has diverged considerably from the original Australian stock, whereas the pukeko is from a very recent Holocene migration and is indistinguishable from Australian forms.

Older land-bird migrants to New Zealand became modified in various ways, the most notable being flightlessness and giantism. In most environments flight is of prime importance, allowing birds to escape predators and nest in the comparative safety of trees. The necessity of flight has tended to restrict the size of birds since flight is naturally a lot easier for small light birds. However, the New Zealand environment, without flesh-eating predators, tended to encourage flightlessness and also the development of ground-nesting habits. Loss of flight in turn paved the way to giantism, and as the birds became larger other changes occurred: the feathers grew heavier and sparser, the legs stouter and shorter, and the brain became relatively small in relation to the beak, jaws and cheek muscles. This was a response to the adoption of a grazing habit, like grazing animals elsewhere in the world. The takahe, kakapo and extinct goose (*Cnemiornis*) are examples of late Cenozoic land-bird migrants that became larger and flightless, whereas the New Zealand robins, for example, became larger without completely losing the power of flight.

Trans-Tasman migration of Australian land birds continues unabated today and colonists arriving in the past century include the spur-wing plover, black-fronted dotterel, white-faced heron, Australian coot, royal spoonbill, grey teal, welcome swallow and waxeye. Other would-be colonists have lingered but not survived — for example the avocet, little bittern and the white-eyed duck.

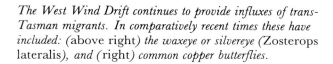

The West Wind Drift continues to provide influxes of trans-Tasman migrants. In comparatively recent times these have included: (above right) *the waxeye or silvereye (*Zosterops lateralis*), and* (right) *common copper butterflies.*

The New Zealand fantail and kingfisher, although similar to the Australian forms, are slightly different and for these changes to have occurred have probably been in New Zealand for some time.

Of these natural colonists the smallest is the waxeye (or silvereye) *(Zosterops lateralis)*, now found throughout New Zealand from sea level to 1,000 metres. The spread of these lively and attractive colonists was well documented by early naturalists. The first invading waxeyes reached southern Westland or Southland in the 1830s; by 1856 they had become established in Canterbury and Nelson, then in 1862 they crossed Cook Strait, reaching Wanganui in 1863, Auckland in 1865 and the Bay of Islands by 1867. The spread of the waxeye did not stop there, and by 1904 it had reached Norfolk Island and the Chatham Islands about 1861. By some strange chance, however, the Kermadec Islands were either missed or proved unsuitable. In 1874 waxeyes were found on lonely inhospitable Campbell Island and in 1904 Scott's Antarctic expedition found them to be the most abundant bird on the Auckland Islands.

The Kaikoura Orogeny

The trans-Tasman migrants of the mid-Cenozoic times arrived in New Zealand to find a land with a wide range of maritime climates and ecological niches. Yet although there were many signs that the land was stirring, there was still no evidence of truly mountainous terrain and instead a long narrow-gutted land had formed, giving rise to hill country — the first in over 50 million years — in Marlborough, Wairarapa and Murchison. This, then, formed the backbone of the new country, foreshadowing the development of the modern main ranges of both the North and South Islands. At the same time, thick layers of gravel, boulders and scree (Great Marlborough Conglomerate) were being deposited in valleys such as the Clarence Valley after having been eroded off the infant Inland and Seaward Kaikouras, then starting to be pushed up to either side. Elsewhere, andesite volcanic chains were active on land in the Coromandel Peninsula and around Dunedin, and volcanic islands were erupting in north Taranaki and on the site of the modern Banks Peninsula.

During Pliocene times (5–2 million years ago) Australia and New Zealand continued to travel in tandem northwards, moving at a rate of about six centimetres per year (i.e. at about twice the rate fingernails grow). This northwards migration moved Australia further and further into the latitudes of hot and tropical climates and New Zealand into those of warm-temperate and subtropical latitudes. The timing of this northwards movement can be obtained from traces of ancient dust storms preserved in layers of sediment laid down in the Tasman Sea off the coast of Australia. Samples obtained by deep-sea drilling show that dust storms first began in the middle

75

Miocene in northern Australia, indicating the onset of desert conditions. As Australia continued to drift north the desert zones extended southwards until in the early Pliocene they had a similar distribution to those of today.

At the same time, major earth movements that in most instances have continued to modern times, began all around the Pacific. A circum-Pacific 'mobile belt' or 'ring of fire' was produced, characterised by earthquakes and volcanoes that were to eventuate in the creation of the mountain chains that today fringe the Pacific. During this time, the mountainous backbones of Japan and New Zealand were formed, as were the Rockies and Andes of the Americas and their continuations through Central America.

We now arrive at the making of modern New Zealand, when those features that today we so readily identify as defining this country were formed. It was during this time that the present shape and topography of our islands were fleshed out. The axial ranges were formed — the earth movements most acute in a belt trending from East Cape obliquely south-westward through the Southern Alps to Fiordland, and decreasing towards the more stable districts of Northland-Auckland in the north and Otago-Stewart Island to the south. And the name we give to this sustained phase of mountain-building is the Kaikoura Orogeny, so-called after the mountains it created. What's more, the orogeny continues unabated today, constantly shaping and redefining our landscape. We live in its ominous shadow and it is the stuff from which our history is made. Wellington in 1855, Tarawera in 1886, Napier in 1931 — these are the tragic events that mark a nation's history.

How then did this prodigious phase of mountain-building eventuate? As with the early Miocene, the movements of this period result from the convergence of the Indian-Australian and Pacific Plates. It will be recalled that during the Miocene as Australia and New Zealand were being shunted north by the wedge of new sea floor forming in the Southern Ocean, the New Zealand block was also being skewed counter-clockwise so that a crack had developed in the Pacific Plate. This crack would eventually become a plate boundary, progressively extending along what is now the Macquarie Ridge and into southern New Zealand until it traversed the entire country as the Alpine Fault and its northern branches. By about 23 million years ago New Zealand found itself astride a zone of subduction with the edge of the Indian-Australian Plate being pushed over the oceanic Pacific Plate. Immense buckling, shearing and faulting resulted as the crust of this zone was caught as if between the jaws of a vast vice. Initially, the uplift would have been minor; only later when the plate boundary shifted north into New Zealand were the movements associated with the Alpine Fault initiated, culminating in the uplift of the Southern Alps during the Pliocene, 5–2 million years ago.

Today the Alpine Fault is said to be one of the few faults visible from space. Over 600 kilometres long in a virtually straight line from Milford Sound to the Spencer Mountains in Nelson, the fault dramatically marks the point where the Indian-Australian Plate over-rides its Pacific counterpart. The resulting collision has not only thrust up our alpine ranges but has also ripped apart the crust, shunting it sideways for hundreds of kilometres. Where once rocks lay side by side, now they are 450 kilometres apart, so that rocks of the 'red hills' in Otago on the eastern side of the fault are precisely matched by 'red hills' in Nelson on the western side.

Calculating the actual rate of uplift is more problematic and all we can say is that the uplift and the formation of the Southern Alps have been occurring at

The aftermath of the quake: the corner of King and Heretaunga Streets, Hastings, 1931. Such events testify to the fact that the Kaikoura Orogeny continues today.

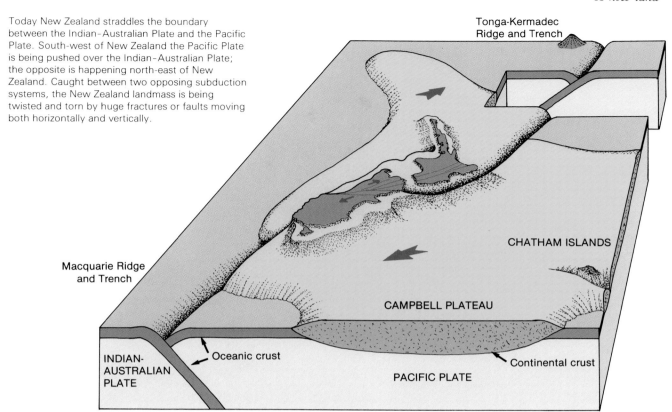

Today New Zealand straddles the boundary between the Indian-Australian Plate and the Pacific Plate. South-west of New Zealand the Pacific Plate is being pushed over the Indian-Australian Plate; the opposite is happening north-east of New Zealand. Caught between two opposing subduction systems, the New Zealand landmass is being twisted and torn by huge fractures or faults moving both horizontally and vertically.

Tonga-Kermadec Ridge and Trench

CHATHAM ISLANDS

Macquarie Ridge and Trench

CAMPBELL PLATEAU

INDIAN-AUSTRALIAN PLATE

Oceanic crust

Continental crust

PACIFIC PLATE

different rates, probably increasing towards the present day. The danger is taking a known rate of uplift and extending it over the life of the orogeny. Thus, although an uplift rate of 10.7 metres per 1,000 years is known from the Alpine Fault near Paringa River, Westland, for the last 10,000 years since the end of the Ice Age, such a rate, if continued for 3 million years, would provide 32,100 metres of uplift — making the Southern Alps the highest ranges in the world! (Everest is by comparison only 8,848 metres high.)

Clearly, erosion alone cannot account for the disparity between such calculated rates of uplift and the actual height of the Southern Alps, and since evidence suggests that the tempo of the Kaikoura Orogeny has been increasing towards the present day, the observed post-Ice Age rates should not be extrapolated to the beginning of the Kaikoura Orogeny in Pliocene times. Nonetheless, uplift of the Southern Alps has been substantial and rapid — certainly of the order of at least 18,600 metres judging from rocks altered by heat and pressure at great depths and now exposed at the surface. Wind, rain and frost have subsequently done their job so that now Mt Cook is a more modest 3,704 metres above sea level.

It was also during the Pliocene that the characteristic 'basin and range' topography in many parts of New Zealand was produced. This resulted when some blocks of country were pushed up faster than others. In Nelson and northern Westland the Murchison, Grey-Inangahua and Nelson, depressions lie between uplifted blocks. Similarly in Central Otago, movements have pushed up a series of ranges — for example, the Rock and Pillar Range (1,450 metres) and Pisa Range (1,960 metres) — each separated by depressions. This part of the country is also notable for its vast stretches of peneplain landscape,

exhumed from beneath its former cover of marine sediments, and it is this surface that has been broken to produce the basins and ranges of today. The Southern Alps have also been cut out of the old peneplain surface, as shown by the fact that many peaks come up to about the same height ('summit accordance'), indicating a common plane of origin.

In the North Island, away from the axial ranges and the sites of faulting, other equally dramatic events were underway. Where the Indian-Australian Plate was over-riding the Pacific Plate the crust was being stretched and pulled, and a zone of swarming earthquakes racked the crust which began to subside in a trough-like depression, particularly in the Taupo-Rotorua district. As the Pacific Plate descended deeper and deeper into the mantle, it encountered progressively hotter temperatures until eventually the rocks comprising the plate melted, generating vast quantities of molten magma. This in turn worked its way upwards through the cracks or conduits formed by the crust's stretching, erupting on the surface as volcanoes. In this way the characteristic volcanic cones of much of the central North Island were formed.

Taranaki has had a long history of andesite volcanic activity, related to magmas generated from the deepest parts of the down-dipping Benioff Zone underlying the central North Island. Taranaki volcanism began in late Pliocene or early Pleistocene, 1.75 million years ago, when the Sugar Loaves and Paritutu were volcanoes, and progressed through centres at Kaitake (575,000 years ago), Pouakai (240,000 years ago) and lastly Egmont (which began erupting 70,000 years ago) — all in line and 8-10 kilometres apart. The latest eruptions of Egmont occurred in AD 1500, AD 1604, AD 1665 and AD 1755, so that volcanic activity is certainly still in the 'dormant'

Gradual movement along the Alpine Fault, spread over many millions of years, has torn New Zealand's South Island in two. Rocks that were once adjacent have moved for a distance of some 450 km. The diagram on the right depicts the situation before movement took place (some say about 140 million years ago, others 9 million years ago). The diagram on the far right depicts the situation as it is today.

Rocks younger than 167 million years

Rocks 345–167 million years old

Rocks originally deposited 345–167 million years ago but now altered by heat and pressure.

Rocks older than 345 million years

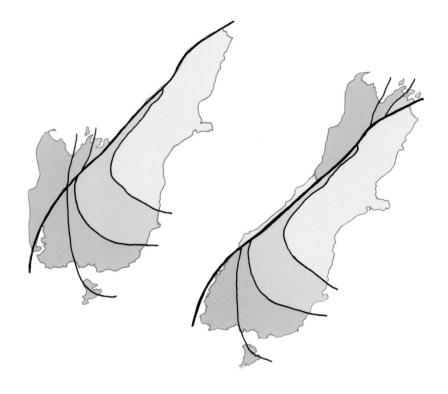

GR

stage and *not* 'extinct'. The next eruption may continue the trend-line towards the south, and a new cone *may* form near Kaponga in south-west Taranaki. Alternatively, Egmont may one day blow its top off, devastating a very wide area. Although this latter possibility is not considered likely, it should not be ignored — hence the need for systems of volcanic surveillance.

In the centre of the North Island, Tongariro and Ruapehu are both volcanoes that have lost their tops in explosions — Tongariro having been reduced virtually to a stump. Activity at Tongariro is probably in a dying phase, but Ruapehu is still going strong. Both Tongariro and Ruapehu date back to early and middle Pleistocene time, whereas Ngauruhoe is a comparative youngster, being only 2,500 years old. Ngauruhoe has had two major eruptive episodes lately: 1948–49 and 1954–55. However, although most spectacular, the lava flows and ash emissions accompanying these eruptions did not pose any significant danger. In January and March 1974 and February 1975 Ngauruhoe erupted incandescent material but no lava.

On the other hand, Ruapehu's crater lake poses a substantial risk, as even very slight activity can send vast quantities of debris-laden water roaring down the volcanic slopes. Immense flood avalanches and mudflows (called 'lahars') have been a feature of previous activity and if one occurs in the future extensive damage may extend down valleys from the volcano all the way to the sea. In 1953 a lahar carried away the Tangiwai railway bridge and 151 people died when a crowded express train plunged through the gap soon after. In April 1975 a small lahar covered part of the ski field and demolished two small buildings, fortunately without loss of life.

Elsewhere in the Taupo-Rotorua region 163 basalt and andesite volcanic vents have been identified, and many more are probably concealed beneath the vast sheets of ignimbrite (welded volcanic particles, deposited by fiery cloud eruptions). Some 12-16,000 cubic kilometres (4,000 cubic miles) of material has been erupted from the Taupo-Rotorua zone during the past 1–1½ million years. The ejection of such large quantities of material from beneath has caused repeated subsidence of the surface — leading to the formation of the present volcanic trough (or graben). The last major outburst from the Taupo-Rotorua region was in AD 130, although smaller eruptions occurred in AD 500, 700 and 1020. Tarawera erupted in 1886 and White Island is continuously active.

Elsewhere, the geology of the North Island is also defined by volcanism. In the Miocene and Pliocene Coromandel Peninsula was the site of a volcanic arc similar to that of the modern Rotorua-Taupo arc. It is thought by some scientists that this line of volcanism through Coromandel marked the New Zealand plate boundary at this time. However, in the late Pliocene and early Pleistocene the Coromandel region, along with Auckland and Northland, was rotated away from the plate boundary, giving the characteristic twist to the North Island's shape. Volcanism thus gradually died out in Coromandel and the volcanic arc was then propagated through the Rotorua-Taupo region.

In Northland geological mapping has shown that at least 26 volcanoes have been active at various times

FAR LEFT: *From the air, the Alpine Fault is here clearly distinguishable on the north-west side of the Awatere Valley.* LEFT: *The sustained upthrust of the Southern Alps reaches its apex in the Westland/Mt Cook region. From Mt Tasman (left) the huge icefields of the Fox, Franz Josef and Tasman glaciers radiate east and west of the Main Divide.* BELOW: *The coastline north of Cape Turakirae, Wellington. Since the fifteenth century earthquakes have raised the beaches eight metres.*

GR

GR

79

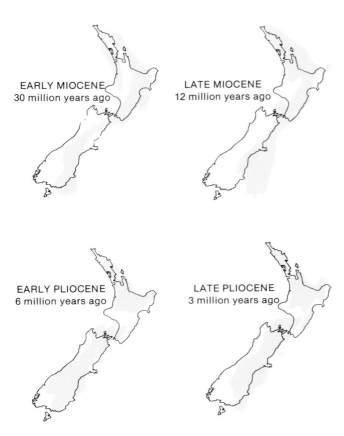

EARLY MIOCENE
30 million years ago

LATE MIOCENE
12 million years ago

EARLY PLIOCENE
6 million years ago

LATE PLIOCENE
3 million years ago

mainly around the Bay of Islands and Whangarei since the late Pliocene, 3 million years ago. Te Puke, the youngest volcano, erupted between AD 200–700. In the Auckland metropolitan region at least 50 volcanoes have erupted over the last 50,000 years, and Rangitoto, the youngest, was last active between 750 and 150 years ago. As far as future volcanic risk is concerned, both Northland and Auckland should certainly be regarded as 'dormant' rather than 'extinct' volcanic regions, and there is every possibility that new cones may appear in the next 500–1,000 years.

Today the subduction zone continues to define the geology of the North Island. As the floor of the Pacific Ocean descends down under the North Island, great thicknesses of sea floor muds and sands are scraped off by the edge of the land. The hard rocks along the leading edge of the North Island act rather like a huge bulldozer and the muds and sands are piled up. This scraping-off process extending over at least the last 20 million years has created a strip of land made up of crumpled and broken sedimentary layers that continues along the entire length of the eastern coastline from East Cape to Kaikoura. Furthermore, marine surveys have shown that similar land is in the making in a region extending for some distance immediately offshore. Broken, crumpled and intensely folded and faulted sediments extend offshore some 120 kilometres beyond the present coastline, to the edge of the Hikurangi Trough. In time, this material will in its turn be piled up and pushed up and added as a broad strip of new land to the east coast of New Zealand. However, we will probably have to wait some 5 or 10

million years or longer for the full width of the presently submerged strip of the new land to emerge as usable real estate! In the meantime, the East Coast provides one of the most dramatic examples anywhere in the world of geological forces in the process of building a new piece of land.

A new ecology

We return now to Pliocene times, 3–4 million years ago, to when the Kaikoura Orogeny was getting into its full stride.

As the ranges were rising, world sea level was rising also, probably in response to changing ocean basins, in turn a reflection of continental drift and sea-floor spreading. Thus in the late Pliocene many areas of New Zealand were submerged for the very last time. The Southern Alps were high enough at that time to stand above the waters, but much of the North Island was inundated and marine straits crossed sags in the then quite low main ranges at the sites of the modern Manawatu Gorge and Kuripapango (Hawke's Bay). Cook Strait first came into being during this transgression — the sea then flooding in over a low-lying break in New Zealand's mountainous backbone (probably the site of a cross-cutting fault system). Similarly, in the far north, beyond Ahipara, the coastline now occupied by the Ninety Mile Beach was covered by sea which also flowed across the Auckland Isthmus, from the Hauraki Gulf to Manukau Harbour.

Despite this, the steady uplift of land had created a fairly continuous northeast-southwest landmass with a backbone of mountainous terrain. The presence of this land barrier now accentuated climatic differences between the east and west coasts of both islands. The west coast tended to be influenced by warm water carried south from Australia by the East Australian Current, whereas the east coast became susceptible to the chilling effects of the Antarctic winds and currents. A range of ecological niches now evolved, often in close proximity to each other but separated by mountain barriers, so that while the west coast was still receiving such northern migrants as the Australian wattles and blue gums, the climate was decidedly more temperate. As well, coastal and lowland environments were now giving way to montane and subalpine ecologies.

As our mountains were pushed up, certain plants and animals moved up with them — especially those adapted to life in dry stony river beds and rocky slopes — and populated the newly created subalpine and alpine areas. Thus the alpine rock wren, alpine wetas and alpine cicadas were developed from lowland groups. In this way the kea (*Nestor notabilis*), a cheeky inhabitant of the South Island high country, developed from the same stock as the kaka, now living in lowland forests.

And then about 2.4 million years ago all these events were overshadowed by climatic changes first started far to the south and generated by the Antarctic continent. The continental sheet and sea ice that had gradually been building up for 30 million years now reached a critical point, triggering a massive cooling phase. The Ice Age had arrived.

FAR LEFT: *Although most of the volcanoes of the central North Island are andesitic, the geothermal activity of the Rotorua region is rhyolitic.* LEFT: *Mt Ruapehu. The incised bank in the foreground reveals a cross-section of the various ash layers deposited during the different eruptive episodes.* BELOW: *The* kea (Nestor notabilis), *found mainly in the forest ranges to the west of the Southern Alps, moved up with the mountains when they were pushed up during the Kaikoura Orogeny.*

6. The Ice Age

About 2.4 million years ago the build-up of polar ice triggered a cooling phase, plunging the world into a sustained ice age that ended only 10,000 years ago; today its imprint shapes our modern landscape.

Pliocene	Pleistocene	Holocene
	2 m.y.a.	10,000 y.a.

THE 'Ice Age' is a term familiar to most people. It conjures up pictures of desolate frozen wastes, mammoths and stone-age humans. But this is only one aspect of the period geologists call the Pleistocene, which together with the Holocene (the last 10,000 years) make up the Quaternary Era, spanning roughly the last 2.4 million years. Apart from its popular appeal, the Pleistocene is of great importance in human terms because it spans the greater part of the period of human evolution and largely produced the scenery we now enjoy, the fertile soils on which we depend, and the flora and fauna which we both compete with and exploit.

Despite its name, there was more to the 'Ice Age' than its icy-cold climates and great advancing ice sheets. Although there were periods of intense cold, when ice sheets and glaciers pushed and scoured their way across large areas of the globe, the cold periods (or glacials) were punctuated by times when climate improved to such an extent that temperatures at any one place could be as genial or more so than they are now. These warm periods are known as interglacials.

Similarly, it would be wrong to imagine a cataclysm, some dreadful event which first plunged the world into a frozen frigid wilderness. There was no sudden dramatic change in the world's climate. Instead, the events that shaped the Ice Age began 130 million years ago with the break up of Gondwana and Laurasia. As the supercontinents broke up, land was rotated into the high latitudes of the globe until eventually Antarctica virtually straddled the South Pole, and the North Pole became hemmed in by cold lands. These continental movements — bringing more land into the polar regions and creating land-encircled areas of ocean that through a lack of circulation could become extremely cold — created the right conditions for the build-up of ice sheets and the lowering of global temperatures. About 45 million years ago the world's climate began to deteriorate. By about 2.4 million years ago, a major cooling occurred, triggering a massive phase of ice build-up, and the first of a series of at least 12 glacial episodes began. These continued until about 850,000 years ago.

As time passed the effects of the Ice Age deepened. Between 850,000 years ago and 14,000 years ago there were at least eight further glacial episodes. These were of much longer duration than the ones that had preceded them and this shift from many small to a few large episodes is thought to have been triggered by the extension of permanent ice sheets to cover the entire Arctic Ocean, and by the spread of pack ice outwards from the Antarctic ice cap to cover vast areas of the Southern Ocean. Increasing amounts of ice now piled up on the land, and the glacial periods became prolonged and intensified.

During a glacial episode, as more and more snow and ice builds up on the surface of the earth it reflects more and more of the sun's heat out into space. This heat disappears into space and is permanently lost to the earth. The more the earth cools, the more ice sheets thicken and grow to cover more and more of the earth's surface. The growing ice sheets push more pack ice and icebergs into the oceans and so cool the water. Changes of sea level accompanying the build-up of ice affect the distribution of land areas and this in turn affects air and oceanic currents and snow and ice formation. Once a period of cold has been started it tends to be intensified and perpetuated by its own physical effects. But a turning point is eventually reached, possibly resulting from fluctuations in solar energy, atmospheric carbon dioxide, or the tilting of the earth's axis, and a period of warming-up starts.

As melting begins to outpace the addition of new snow, the spread of ice stops. The ice sheets gradually thin, and the ice slowly begins to withdraw. As the climate becomes warmer, plants and animals migrate into areas abandoned by the shrinking ice sheet. The hardiest, or those able to spread most rapidly, come first. Meanwhile the ice dwindles and vanishes, or perhaps only a few mountain glaciers and isolated ice caps are left. We are now in an interglacial. But eventually, with the continuing swing of the pendulum, the climate will deteriorate and once more ice will accumulate. In this way, Pleistocene climates oscillated between cold glacials and warm interglacials.

The climates of the interglacial periods were frequently as warm as that of the present-day, or warmer; and the remains of many warmth-loving plants and animals are found in interglacial deposits that were laid down in latitudes far beyond their present day range. For example, populations of the hippopotamus were able to move across temporarily dry parts of the Mediterranean and the North Sea to gain entry into the British Isles. In New Zealand the climate warmed up to such an extent during at least some of the interglacials that kauri forests and bright red subtropical soils, suggesting subtropical vegetation, extended as far south as Wellington.

Although the actual extent of the ice sheets varied considerably from one ice age to another, we know that about 20,000 years ago, at the height of the last glacial, ice covered some 27 per cent of the earth's land surface, compared with less than 10 per cent today. In the Northern Hemisphere extensive ice sheets formed on the land. An ice sheet centred on Scandinavia pushed southwards across northern Europe, extending as far south as a line drawn through Amsterdam, Dresden, Krakow, Lvov, Kiev, Kharkov and Kazan. Ice sheets covered the Urals and Siberia. The European mountain chains had their own ice sheets. In Britain ice pushed down from Scotland, the Lake District, Wales and central Ireland to cover all the British Isles except that part south of a line drawn between London and Bristol. Large parts of both the Irish Sea and the North Sea were dry land and extensively covered with ice. In North America thick ice sheets scoured their way southwards to cover all of Canada and eventually pushed south into the middle states of the USA. South of the main North American continental ice sheets ice caps developed on the higher mountain ranges.

Elsewhere in the world ice formed on the mountains of South America, Africa, Australia and New Zealand. Extensive areas of floating pack ice and icebergs blocked the Arctic and North Atlantic seas and pushed out on all sides from the massive ice caps on Antarctica.

The difference in mean annual temperature between glacial and interglacial episodes was about 14°C. Where a region is already covered with ice and snow, further cooling has little obvious effect and similarly, where the climate is already tropical a small drop in temperature may affect vegetation and perhaps rainfall, but otherwise little else. However, in most mid-latitude lands, where climate is 'temperate' and delicately balanced between hot and cold, the drop in temperature associated with the change from an interglacial to a glacial climate tipped the climatic balance in a most dramatic way. Middle latitude lands like New Zealand experienced a considerable swing in climate; many parts of the country passing from temperate conditions (or subtropical during the peaks of interglacials) to those more like the harsh treeless alpine and subalpine regions of today. However, the moderating influence of the sea meant that the overall effects of glacial climates were not quite so severe in New Zealand, compared with those of continental Europe and North America.

Periglacial climates

Although most people are undoubtedly familiar with glaciers and ice sheets because they are glamorous and photogenic, less familiar and decidedly unglamorous are the diverse range of landscape forms developed in the zone surrounding a glacial area.

In any glacial the actual areas occupied by the glaciers themselves are comparatively small compared with those areas affected by the harsh climates imposed

Pack ice, Ross Sea, Antarctica. About 2.4 million years ago the expansion of the polar ice sheets triggered off a complex series of climatic changes, leading to a massive build-up of global ice.

on the surrounding regions. The area affected by a frost climate, which is often (but not necessarily) peripheral to a glaciated area, is called the periglacial zone.

The effects of freeze and thaw, related to harsh frost climates, exerted a pervasive influence on many of the Ice Age landscapes. As a climate deteriorates at the beginning of a glacial period vast tracts of forest are depleted and eventually killed off. In its place areas of bare rock and soil are exposed. Vegetated areas are sparse and consist of thin covers of herbs, small hardy shrubs and grasses. Often the vegetation cover gives little, if any, protection to the underlying soils and rocks.

Although in most glacial areas there is little if any rain and most of the precipitation falls as snow and ice, a certain amount of thawing occurs during daytime as temperatures rise and running melt water is often locally quite abundant. Such water penetrates deeply into the exposed or poorly covered soil and rock. During the night as temperatures fall, the melt water freezes and the ice that forms in the soil and rock exerts a wedging effect. Where water has penetrated a hairline crack in a rock, on freezing it forms a series of minute ice crystals along the line of the crack. As the crystals grow they act like a tiny wedge, forcing the sides of the crack apart. Ice crystals growing in soils exert similar pressures, leading to fragmentation of the soil (frost heave).

The daily cycle of freeze and thaw continuing over many millennia during glacial phases wrought enormous changes in the landscape. Bare rock surfaces were shattered to considerable depths and the material prised loose by the wedging effects of freeze and thaw tumbled downslope as fragments so that hilly areas became fringed by extensive aprons of rock and soil debris — talus fans, rock glaciers, debris flows, etc. Soils on steeply sloping terrain were disrupted by frost heave and slid downhill as mud glaciers, leaving behind bare rock surfaces, to be in turn attacked by frost action. On more gently sloping or flat surfaces, the daily cycles of frost heave subjected the soils to a sorting process during which coarse and fine materials were segregated into heaps or strips — producing 'patterned ground'.

Sometimes the soils, particularly those that had developed to some depth, were affected by a process called solifluxion (*solum*:soil; *fluere*:flow). Most soils developed under a temperate climate are reasonably free-draining and water does not normally accumulate within the soil. But with the onset of periglacial conditions the water in the soil freezes and in deep soils may form impermeable layers of ice in the subsoil beneath the surface. This ice in the subsoil largely remains frozen all year round, although substantial melting and thinning of the frozen layers may occur in summer. In the uppermost level of

RM

84

the subsoil, and more particularly in the overlying soil layers, daytime warmth is able to penetrate to some depth and, when temperatures rise above freezing, all the melt water accumulates in the top layers of soil but is prevented from draining away through the soil by the presence of deeper layers of frozen ground. Saturated with water, the soil becomes unstable and begins to flow downhill, coming to rest as a mantle of debris.

The daily cycle of freezing and thawing also acts on the constituents of the soil. Small rock fragments are progressively broken down to yield sand grains and clay particles, and larger rock fragments are split into many angular pieces. When combined with the melt water this produces a highly mobile porridge-like mass, composed of mud and angular fragments of rock. The saturated mass readily slides downhill as mudflows and tongues of chaotic debris, filling in the existing valleys and fringing the slopes of the hills with debris. During its downhill slide the angular material carried within the solifual debris is dragged across the underlying rocks. Its erosive action can be likened to a rock version of a glacier and as it moves it bulldozes the soil off the slopes. The sandpaper-like effect of the moving debris tends to 'shave' the underlying rock surfaces so that today we can see solid rock overlain by a deposit of coarse angular rock debris set in a silty matrix, the junction between the two being extremely sharp, without any sign of gradation (the junction is called a 'shaved surface').

Falling sea levels

The build-up of snow and ice on the land locked up vast amounts of water that otherwise would have found its way back to the sea. Each glacial period was, therefore, accompanied by a substantial lowering of world sea levels. As the ice caps increased in extent and thickness, so the sea level gradually dropped. During the coldest phase of the last glacial period (25,000–15,000 years ago), the world sea level was 120–135 metres lower than it is now, and it may have dropped even further to reach some 165 metres below today's sea level. It was during the early part of the last glacial period, about 40,000 years ago, when the sea level was low, that the ancestors of the Aborigines were able to move from South-East Asia across Indonesia into Australia.

The worldwide drops in sea level drastically altered the shapes of many of the present landmasses. Britain, for example, was joined to France, Belgium, Holland and Germany across what is now the North Sea. The Bering Strait was dry and formed a land bridge for animal migrations between Asia and America. The myriad of islands in Indonesia were all connected by land and linked

LEFT: *In the periglacial zone melt water cascades down a mountainside in a daily cycle of freezing and thawing.* BELOW: *Melt water mixes with soil and rock debris eroded from the Fox Glacier. In the background alluvial fans coalesce at the base of the riverbank.*

to the mainland of South-East Asia. Around the New Zealand coast the retreating sea exposed wide areas of sea floor. The North and South Islands were joined across Cook Strait, and Stewart Island was linked across Foveaux Strait to Southland. In the Auckland region the large coastal inlets such as Hokianga, Kaipara, Manukau, Waitemata, Raglan and Kawhia harbours were dry land, as was the Hauraki Gulf and the Firth of Thames.

In New Zealand the ice started to retreat about 14,000 years ago. However, in many parts of the world ice sheets lingered on until 10,000 years ago, and in fact there was a marked cold episode between 11,000 and 10,000 years ago, so that this latter date is often taken as the 'official' end of the last glacial. It also marks the end of the Pleistocene period, or Ice Age, and the beginning of the Holocene. As the climate warmed and the ice sheets melted, the sea rose from its low glacial levels (120–150 metres below present sea level) to reach about 35 metres below its modern height 10,000 years ago. In the period between 10,000 and 6,500 years ago as the ice sheets continued to melt the sea rose at a rate that often exceeded 10 millimetres per year, until about 6,500 years ago it had reached a level close to that of the present. The last remnants of the Scandinavian ice sheet had melted by 7,000 years ago, and those of the North American ice sheet by 6,500 years ago. As the climate continued to improve, the sea level steadily rose, until 5,000–4,000 years ago, when warm temperatures peaked (the Climatic Optimum), it reached a height about two metres above the present sea level, presumably in response to a thinning of the existing world's ice caps, such as those in Antarctica, Greenland, Scandinavia and North Canada. Since then the sea has dropped to its present level.

No more ice ages?

We may ask if the Ice Age has now ended. Have we seen the final glacial period, and are we now moving towards a more equable worldwide climate? Or are we heading closer and closer to a new cold period?

Evidence suggests that the present global climatic patterns are not the normal patterns of the geological ages in the past but are very much a hang-over from the Ice Age. For much of the vast length of geological time before the Pleistocene, there were no ice caps, and the world was divided up into only two, or at the most three, broad climatic zones: an extensive tropical/subtropical zone and an equally extensive temperate zone. Occasionally, depending on where the world's landmasses were located, and the configuration of ocean currents, the temperate zone may have been subdivided into warm-temperate and cool- or cold-temperate.

The present climatic pattern, consisting of a number of relatively narrow climatic zones, ranging from tropical to polar, is related almost entirely to the presence of ice caps at both the North and South poles. On this basis alone it is thought we are now in an interglacial and that we have not seen the last of severe glacial climates. Also, because we have already passed the Climatic Optimum, when warm temperatures peaked following the end of

the last glacial period, we may be on the downward slope, heading towards a new ice age. However, we can console ourselves with the knowledge that any cooling of climate will take the form largely of a virtually imperceptible general trend downwards, averaging out over a whole series of ups and downs of warmer and colder phases. Also, any changes that might occur in the future will be incredibly slow in terms of the human lifespan.

Judging from cores obtained from both the sea floor and the Arctic and Antarctic ice caps, it is the Southern Hemisphere which leads the way into an ice age, with the Northern Hemisphere lagging some 3,000 years behind. According to some scientists the Antarctic region has gone more than halfway back from its most recent climatic high point towards the conditions of a full ice age and, although the Northern Hemisphere has not yet caught up, we can expect a global ice age to begin in the near future, perhaps within about 1,000 years.

In the meantime many scientists believe that climate will fluctuate and we will have little troughs and peaks — and perhaps another 'Little Ice Age' — before plunging into the next glacial that is calculated to continue through to 119,000 years from now. If we are on our way back into an ice age, just a small deterioration will put an intolerable strain on our capacity to feed our expanding populations. In this way, Nature, by a small change, could destroy the habitats of millions of humans. Climatic change, therefore, presents a major challenge — perhaps the major challenge — to civilisation.

New Zealand on ice

In New Zealand the Ice Age began with a marked cooling of the seas at about 2.4 million years ago. As the climate deteriorated ice began to build up on the high country, particularly in the Southern Alps and Fiordland, rates of erosion accelerated and rivers began to build up their courses. Sequences of river terraces, glacial moraines, peat swamps and successions of marine deposits, both on land and under the sea, document the fact that New Zealand experienced the same dramatic series of yo-yo-like shifts in climate that were such a marked feature of the Pleistocene period or Ice Age elsewhere in the world.

During at least some of the glacial periods Auckland's climate probably changed to match that of Dunedin today, and Wellington experienced frost climates similar to those in northern Norway today. Extensive glaciers formed in the Southern Alps. Along the West Coast these glaciers reached out into the sea. Eastwards the alpine glaciers made their inexorable way down the valleys of the foothills and in some instances joined together to form extensive apron-like ice sheets along the inland flanks of the Canterbury Plains.

Numerous thick ice sheets also developed in Fiordland, and much of its landscape was scoured and over-ridden by ice. As the ice made its way down, vast amounts accumulated around the edges of the Fiordland massif. To the west and south-west great thicknesses of ice pushed out from Fiordland towards the sea (then at a much lower level, at least 120 metres below that of the present day), scouring out deep valleys. With the dis-

The Fox Glacier. Although retreating, the glacier still flows nearly 13 kilometres, descending from the Main Divide of the Southern Alps through temperate rain forest to within a few hundred metres of sea level. ABOVE: *The terminal face of the Fox Glacier.* TOP RIGHT: *The so-called Mount Cook lily (Ranunculus lyalli) — one of the most spectacular of our alpine flowers.*

appearance of the ice and the restoration of modern sea level after the Ice Age, such deep valleys were flooded by the sea to become the majestic fiords of today's landscape.

The enormous amounts of ice flowing eastwards off the flanks of Fiordland spilled out across the landscape of inland Southland and Otago. Like the western margins of Fiordland, the great loads of ice flowing eastwards scoured out the valleys through which they passed. Then, after the Ice Age, water drained into these greatly deepened valleys, filling them and forming the great lakes that comprise today's Southern Lake Country (Te Anau, Manapouri, Wakatipu, Wanaka etc.).

In the North Island Mt Egmont, Tongariro and Ruapehu had ice caps, and a number of small glaciers filled the upper reaches of some of the higher valleys in the Tararua and Ruahine ranges.

South of a line passing through the Waikato and the Bay of Plenty there were widespread areas that experienced during at least some of the glacial episodes a harsh cold climate, with varying degrees of frost. In these areas it was not quite cold enough, nor possibly wet enough, for actual ice sheets to accumulate. However, the cold frosty climate was severe enough to discourage the growth of forest and many areas were either completely bare or were thinly covered with hardy shrubs, grasses, rushes and sedges. As a result of the cold, frosty and often windy climate continuous podocarp forest was restricted largely to the northern part of the North Island. Elsewhere, patches of podocarp forest, and more particularly of beech, occurred in sheltered inland areas and in coastal

situations, well away from the cooling effects of the mountains. Parts of the continental shelves, exposed by falling sea levels during glacial periods, also probably had local forested areas.

The survival of podocarps, in particular, with their supply of fleshy seeds, very attractive to birds and other animals, in turn ensured the survival of many animal species. Some, like the alpine wetas and cicadas, would have adapted to the colder environment and would have changed their habitats accordingly; others would have retreated to small local niches, trapped on sheltered north-facing slopes. There they would have survived, waiting for the return of warmer temperatures. Even today we are reminded of the extreme precariousness and fragility of such communities. One of the best examples is the takahe. Considered extinct for most of this century, it was dramatically rediscovered in 1948 in the Murchison mountains west of Lake Te Anau, where it still maintains a tenuous foothold — its total population numbering less than 200. Although its original depletion resulted from the competition and predation from introduced species, the takahe nevertheless demonstrates how small communities of animals would have responded to the change of climate with the onset of a glacial. During summer the takahe feeds on the succulent leaf-bases of tussock, mountain daisy and on various tussock and grass seeds. In winter when snow blankets the grasslands, it retreats into the adjoining beech forest to feed on herbs and ferns. In the same way, animal populations would have retreated and adapted to the changing conditions during a glacial cycle.

ANDRIS APSE LTD

Lake Tekapo and Godley River, Mackenzie Country. In the centre the incised Godley River skirts the flanks of an inclined outwash gravel plain, probably laid down during the late Otiran glacial, 20,000–18,000 years ago. During the height of the last Ice Age much of New Zealand would have resembled this scene.

With the improvement in the climate, forest would have extended out from these various patchy remnants to re-establish itself over much of New Zealand, only to be pushed back again by the onset of another glacial period. Similarly, in the last 14,000 or 10,000 years since the end of the Ice Age, the present forest vegetation, along with its accompanying animal life, has staged a comeback from such areas.

The last glacial period, spanning the time between 100,000 and 10,000 years ago, saw perhaps some of the most intense episodes of cold climate in the entire Ice Age and has had the most obvious and far-reaching influence on all aspects of our total environment. Yet, as with the Ice Age in general, the last glacial period was not all entirely cold and there were fluctuations of climate within the last glacial period, cold phases (stadials) alternating with warm phases (interstadials). There were at least three warm interstadials, separated by cold stadials.

During the three warm interstadials forest occupied much of both the North and South Islands of New Zealand. The cold stadials separating the interstadials were times of very severe climate in New Zealand, during which forest was extremely restricted throughout the country. Substantial areas of New Zealand were probably largely without forest, and in the uplands and over broad swaths of the lowlands the vegetation was dominated by hardy shrubs, herbs and grasses. Isolated patches of beech forest were scattered across the landscape, particularly in sheltered areas. South of the Waikato, the distribution of podocarp forest was extremely fragmented.

The most recent of these cold stadial periods occurred

between 25,000 and 15,000 years ago. During this stadial sea level dropped by 120 metres or more, the sea bed was exposed for often quite considerable distances offshore, and North, South, and Stewart Islands were linked by dry land, as were numerous small offshore islands (Mana, Kapiti, Great Barrier etc.). Mean annual temperatures were at their lowest, and in the South Island massive glaciers extended outwards on all sides from the alpine chain. Ice sheets completely over-rode many of the upland areas of Fiordland and fed glaciers that pushed outwards in all directions. Glaciation was patchy in the northernmost part of the South Island, and consisted of valley glaciers in north-west Nelson, the Spenser and St Arnaud ranges and the Seaward and Inland Kaikouras. In the North Island glaciation was confined to small valley glaciers in the Tararua and southern Ruahine ranges and on the volcanic cones of Egmont, Tongariro and Ruapehu. In the central South Island snowlines were about 830–850 metres lower than those of today, and annual temperatures were lower by about 4.5°C, compared with those of today.

In the South Island and southern parts of the North Island the peak of glaciation was associated with the construction of broad outwash plains by debris-filled rivers and the dumping of layers of wind-blown dust (loess) over much of the eastern side of both islands. Loads of shattered material from the eroding uplands led to massive build-ups in the courses of most of the major river systems, as reflected in spectacular flights of terraces, extensive alluvial plains and massive outwash fans.

Substantial quantities of alluvial material were also

New Zealand in the last glacial phase of the Ice Age (the late Otiran glacial), 20,000–18,000 years ago. The global accumulation of snow and ice on the land locked up vast amounts of water that otherwise would have found its way back to the sea. Each glacial period was, therefore, accompanied by a lowering of world sea levels. As the ice caps increased in extent and thickness so the sea level dropped. During the last glacial period (30,000–20,000 years ago), the world sea level was some 105–135 metres lower than it is now. In New Zealand this resulted in the formation of extensive lowlands in the Taranaki–Cook Strait region, linking the two Islands. As with much of the land, these lowlands were covered in hardy grasses, sedges and shrubs with the occasional pocket of beech forest surviving on the protective northern slopes of hills. Only north of Auckland is it likely that podocarp forests survived.

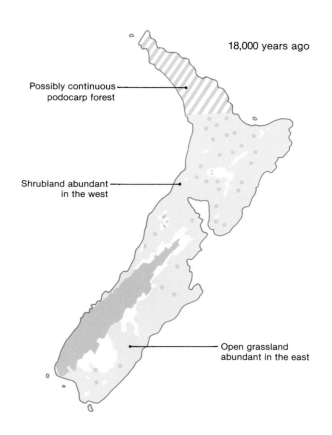

18,000 years ago

Possibly continuous podocarp forest

Shrubland abundant in the west

Open grassland abundant in the east

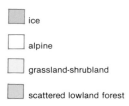

ice

alpine

grassland-shrubland

scattered lowland forest

BELOW: *The Marlborough Sounds. The crenulated coastline of much of modern New Zealand was formed at the end of the last ice age when world sea levels rose as the polar ice caps melted.* RIGHT: *In Fiordland the retreating glaciers scoured out the valleys through which they passed, leaving characteristic U-shaped valleys.* FAR RIGHT: *A typical outwash plain, Mackenzie Country.*

GR

RM

washed out into the sea. There the constant surging to and fro of the waves ground down the material to finer and finer grades. Eventually, the particles of sand, silt and clay produced by such grinding action settled to the sea floor, where they were transported by the waves and piled up around the coasts to form shoals and beach deposits. During low tides and when the sea level itself was low, many of these deposits, exposed to the full force of the icy gales, were stripped off and carried by the wind to considerable distances inland, there to become trapped in vegetation, and to gradually form sand dunes. Large areas of dunes formed in this way are a feature of many New Zealand coastal areas: for example, coastal Taranaki, Manawatu and the Wairarapa.

A result of this constant erosion and dumping during the last glacial has been that a large proportion of our soils date from this time. The abundance of fresh soils, packed with mineral nutrients, ensures fertile growing conditions for a wide range of plants.

Although actual glacial ice was not extensive in the Wellington region, and was apparently largely restricted to valleys high in the Tararua Range, evidence suggests that compared to regions immediately to the north and south, the Wellington region had far more than its fair share of severe climates during the ice ages. During those times the large ice sheets present in many parts of the world generated ferocious wind systems. Because of New Zealand's proximity to the large Antarctic ice cap, and the presence of ice sheets on its own high country, New Zealand would have been constantly buffeted by severe gales, as cold winds howled north up from Antarctica and flowed across the country. These bitterly cold southerly gales, on encountering the New Zealand landmass, and more particularly the high alpine backbone of the Southern Alps, were diverted and channelled along in a north-easterly direction, parallel to the mountains, until they encountered the gap in the Cook Strait region through which they were able to flow.

The effect of high land on either side of the Cook Strait gap was also exaggerated by the glacial fall in sea level of 120–150 metres so that an emormous funnel-like gap was formed in the landscape, channelling and accelerating the freezing air masses moving northwards from the polar regions. The strong and constant winds passing through the Cook Strait gap generated harsh dry conditions throughout the Wellington region. The fierce gales snarling across the landscape confined forest to the most sheltered and climatically favoured sites. Trees were restricted to small patches in a landscape otherwise vegetated by partial coverings of hardy shrubs, herbs and grasses. Elsewhere, the land was stripped virtually bare of vegetation by the continuous glacier-like movements of tongues of debris.

About 14,000 years ago, the climate began to improve quite dramatically and forest began to move back into many upland as well as lowland areas in the North Island. By about 12,000 years ago, all of the North Island except the Wellington region was covered with podocarp-hardwood-dominant forest, and in the South Island shrubland began to replace the previously abundant grasslands. Then about 10,000 years ago a major warming phase led to the rapid expansion of forest in the southern tip of the North Island and in all but the driest eastern districts of the South Island.

BRIAN MOLLOY

7. Postglacial New Zealand

As the ice retreated the surviving plants and animals radiated out, so that within a few centuries vast forests once more covered the land.

Pliocene	Pleistocene	Holocene
	2 m.y.a.	10,000 y.a.

CLOSE to 14,000 years ago the world began to shake off the grip of the last ice age, and by 10,000 years ago was enjoying much warmer conditions. As the ice melted and the earth warmed between 14,000 and 10,000 years ago, the entire global environment — climate, land surface, oceans and biota — was utterly transformed. This period of transformation we call the late glacial. Our present climate, which has lasted since 10,000 years ago, we call the postglacial.

Late glacial: 14,000 to 10,000 years ago

Exactly how the global climate, after thousands of years of constant fluctuations around a cool average temperature, lurched decisively towards a warmer state, no one is sure. A growing network of cores taken from the ocean floor sediments shows that dramatic changes took place at sea as well as on land. These cores contain long records of oxygen isotope variations and marine life, which reveal global changes of total ice volume and sea surface temperatures spanning many thousands of years. Warm interglacials have different patterns of ocean currents and sea surface temperatures to cool glacials. An apron of sea ice 1,000 kilometres north of its present winter boundary extended around Antarctica at the height of the last glacial. In the North Atlantic ice sheets and sea ice deflected major oceanic currents, robbing the high northern latitudes of warm southern water.

Researchers have recently shown that global ice volume is in phase with subtle, but long-term and persistent changes in the seasonal patterns of global solar radiation. These seasonal changes result from orbital variations in the earth's path around the sun. The retreat of the great Northern Hemisphere ice sheets coincided with a period when summer radiation was strong and winter radiation weak at high northern latitudes, which would tend to promote ice melting. However, the actual triggering of the end of the last glacial was probably more complex than that, and may have begun in high southern latitudes. Very recent evidence suggests that increased tilting of the earth's axis affected deep water currents in the oceans, and the amount of CO_2 in the atmosphere. The more CO_2 in the atmosphere, the warmer the earth becomes through the 'greenhouse effect'. The 'greenhouse effect' is a result of the longwave radiation emitted by the earth being trapped in the lower atmosphere. Once the earth's atmosphere began to warm, numerous feedback mechanisms came into play. Most important of these

is the melting of the ice itself. As the ice apron around Antarctica and the vast Northern Hemisphere ice sheets began to shrink the polar caps of bright reflective ice were progressively replaced by duller less reflective water, soil and vegetation. More solar radiation was absorbed, and thus the earth continued to warm.

In the Southern Hemisphere, solar radiation decreased in summer and increased during winter from 18,000 years ago, a minimum seasonal contrast being reached about 11,000 years ago. However, the major effects on the New Zealand climate came from the melting of the Antarctic sea ice. Antarctic sea ice reacted immediately to the changed global conditions and by 14,000 years ago the expanded belt of winter ice retreated to approximately its present position. Warmer waters — pushed north by expanded cool circum-Antarctic waters during the glacial — now returned to envelop the North Island.

With the return of warmer conditions and a dropping away in strength of cold southerly winds, the rate at which snow accumulated in the mountains slowed and ice melting during the summer increased. By 14,000 years ago the glaciers of the South and North islands were in full retreat. As they withdrew they left mountain valleys blocked and infilled with a jumble of bouldery morainic ridges and thick gravel and silt outwash deposits kilometres long. Great fans of debris spread down oversteepened slopes, impounding lakes. The great meandering rivers, loaded with glacial debris, spread silt over their wide gravel beds, and the fierce winds, unimpeded by forest, picked up the dried silt and blew it across the landscape to form thick loess sheets.

Although glaciers had covered only a small proportion of New Zealand, even during the coldest periods of the last glacial, the effects of the cold climate elsewhere on the landscape were as severe. Bare ground and surfaces covered with thin, meagre vegetation were common in all districts south of Auckland until well into the late glacial warming. Such ground was open to heavy frosts and could not absorb the impact of rain, making it prone to erosion. This was as true for the higher altitudes as for lowlands. Shallow soils could not store rainfall and gradually release it so runoff tended to be fast, and flood peaks correspondingly high. Flooding rivers and streams frequently transported enormous quantities of debris, depositing it to fill downstream valleys and to form outwash plains. Silt spread over meandering river channels, was picked up by wind and deposited as loess.

Before 14,000 years ago sparse shrublands and grasslands predominated nearly everywhere. Forest was particularly rare. Only Northland is likely to have had abundant forest. From Auckland southwards, forest survived as small stands, mainly of silver beech, mountain beech and mountain cedar. Otherwise, short to tall shrubland prevailed in hilly regions, and grassland on exposed, open sites and windswept plains. Hilly regions provided shelter, warm north-facing slopes and higher and more consistent rainfall. Dense shrubland and small forest patches were, therefore, more common there than on the plains and rolling country. Tall podocarp forest was exceedingly rare and may have been confined to isolated clumps in climatically favoured, moist, frost-free sites.

From Cook Strait south, even shrubland was restricted and grasslands and herbfield covered the landscape. However, very small patches of forest are almost certain to have survived here also, especially in the climatically favoured north-west Nelson district.

The New Zealand fossil record of terrestrial animal life is much poorer than that of plants. Although plant fossils are abundant and occur in many different sorts of deposits, animal fossils are generally preserved only under special conditions, such as calcareous lake sediments and cave deposits.

Moa bones have been occasionally found in loess deposits, and these large birds were probably capable of using, at least seasonally, the open grasslands and shrublands of the last glacial. Cave deposits which date to the peak of the last glacial have revealed a rich array of bird,

Tussock grassland, Lindis Pass, Central Otago. Before 14,000 years ago sparse shrublands and grasslands covered much of the landscape of both the North and South Islands.

reptile and amphibian remains. There can be no doubt that the restricted areas of forest which surrounded the cave entrances sustained a full range of bird and other animal populations. The glacial forest patches thus contrast starkly with the modern-day equivalents which often have small, species-poor animal populations. There are, however, major differences between the two situations.

Modern forest remnants contain large numbers of mammalian predators, such as rats, cats and pigs, and competitors for plant food such as possums, goats and deer. They are effectively isolated from one another as well, as the intervening countryside is often cultivated or grazed and full of predators.

During the glacial maximum the forest patches, although isolated from other forest areas, were embedded in a landscape covered with shrubland, tall scrub and grassland. Many birds which are primarily forest dwellers — such as kakapo, kiwis, pigeons and tui — are well capable of using other habitats such as shrubland and scrub. For many species the effective size of the forest patches would, therefore, be increased because of the additional resources in the surrounding landscape. The edges of these small forest patches were often on fertile soils and received abundant sunlight, and as a result would have produced large amounts of high-quality forage. Forest edges are preferred habitat for many animals. Small, scattered patches of forest would thus have a greater area of optimal habitat than an equivalent area of unbroken forest.

Similarly, invertebrates are not likely to have been much affected by the reduction in forest extent at the glacial maximum as even small areas of forest can support large populations.

North Island vegetation reacted speedily to the late glacial rise in temperature and rainfall. Tall podocarp forests sprang up almost simultaneously throughout

ABOVE: *A stand of southern beech sheltered in a small sub-montane valley. It is from such pockets that the beech and podocarps re-established themselves at the end of the last glacial.* RIGHT: *In the warm temperate rain forest of the Fox River valley, rata grows alongside tree ferns.* FAR RIGHT: *Rimu forest, Lake Kaniere, Westland.*

northern and central North Island with the exception of western districts from Taranaki south, where grassland-shrublands persisted longer. Shrubland-grassland gave way to tall complex forest in less than 500 years at most locations. The treeline was somewhat lower than it is today, and temperatures were 3-2°C cooler. However, below the prevailing treeline, forest cover was near complete within a few hundred years.

Matai, a tall podocarp tree usually found in districts with fertile soils and dry climates, predominated in lowland forests, but there was a very large range of trees, small trees and subcanopy shrubs present from the very beginning. These late glacial forests were formed from a complex mixture of species now rarely encountered together so that lowland species grew alongside typically subalpine trees such as mountain cedar, silver beech, bog pine and mountain toatoa. This may simply reflect the persistence of the earlier, cold-adapted vegetation, but it may also indicate that cool frosty conditions were still common despite the warmer climate. As the late glacial progressed these cooler elements gradually vanished from northern lowland forests, retreating to higher altitudes as the climate slowly improved.

The speed with which tall forest overtopped and eliminated the late glacial shrubland-grasslands needs explaining. Only small, scattered patches of forest existed before the late glacial warming, and the majority of those were subalpine trees. Nearly all the vast forest of tall podocarp and hardwood trees which sprang up within a few centuries must have stemmed from these groves.

Therefore, small stands of trees, often remote from grassland-covered plains where they were eventually to proliferate, must have multiplied many times within the space of no more than five generations. As most trees can produce many thousands of seeds, and the podocarps are particularly prolific, the problem is not one of seed production but of seed dispersal. Most of the species of tall podocarp forest are bird-dispersed, and shrublands have many species with fruits which attract birds. As we have seen, the isolated patches of forest and shrubland present at the end of the glacial maximum were rich in birds. With the rapid amelioration of the climate, and the rapid increase of nectar-and fruit-bearing trees, bird populations must have expanded at an equally impressive rate. With many birds using shrubland and scrub as well as tall forest — and perhaps moving seasonally between them — opportunities for seed dispersal abounded. Given the huge numbers of birds in New Zealand forests before the introduction of mammalian predators, it may well be that seed dispersal was more effective and rapid than would be suspected on the evidence of our present bird-depleted forests.

By 12,000 years ago tall forest occupied nearly all the North Island, which by now was separated from the South Island by the flooding of Cook Strait as the sea level rose. Only the exposed southern tip of the North Island remained without forest, persisting in shrubland-grassland for nearly 2,000 years longer. With the slow improvement of climate, rimu, tree ferns and many other plants of mild wet climates gradually increased in northern

forests. Low forest or tall podocarp-dominated shrubland steadily extended on to the range crests of the axial ranges and the flanks of the tall central volcanoes.

In the South Island, although the glaciers had reacted speedily to the initial warming 14,000 years ago, the vegetation was slower to respond than its northern counterpart. As the glaciers retreated, grassland and low shrubland advanced from the lowlands to occupy newly bared ground. Nevertheless, although the grasslands and shrublands became more dense and widespread, they still resembled those of the full glacial period. About 12,000 years ago tall shrubland and low forest — mainly of bog pine, mountain toatoa, coprosmas and *Myrsine* — spread into inland mountain valleys abandoned by the now shrunken glaciers. Tussock grassland and low shrubland still prevailed on the drier eastern side of the South Island but on the upper flanks of wetter mountain range daisy, shrubs, coprosmas, *Myrsine*, mountain lacebark and other small trees and shrubs formed dense thickets. Very similar shrubby vegetation covered most of the west coast of the South Island with here and there small patches of broadleaved forest, often dominated by rata and kamahi.

The increased vegetation in the South Island and the expansion of forest and low shrubland into montane and subalpine areas in the North greatly reduced the amount of erosion and lowered flood peaks. River systems began to settle down, abandon their broad flood plains, and cut deep channels. Increased rainfall and more stable rivers allowed deep fertile soils to develop and peat bogs

began to form on poorly drained river terraces and in once dry basins.

The rate of climatic improvement slowed after 12,000 years ago and at some point temperatures may have cooled somewhat as glaciers underwent a resurgence. Rimu and tree-ferns stopped increasing in North Island forests, perhaps indicating somewhat drier conditions as well.

The postglacial revolution

The transition from the full glacial to the climate we know today was by no means a single smooth process, and not all facets of the environment reacted together. However, if any boundary line has to be drawn the date of 10,000 years ago has the best claim. By 10,000 years ago the glaciers had shrunk to their smallest size and the sea level was only 30 metres below the present shore-line. But it was the rapid transformation of the vegetation between 10,500 and 9,500 years ago which marks the end of the glacial and the beginning of our present climate.

In northern forests the last vestiges of cool temperate vegetation vanished from the lowlands. Rimu in the course of a few centuries became the most numerous podocarp in all but the dry south-eastern districts of the North Island. Treeferns, hutu, and other subcanopy trees and shrubs typical of mild, moist climates proliferated. Rata vines were commoner than they have ever been since.

From Cook Strait southwards the landscapes had

95

remained in grassland, shrubland and low forest throughout the late glacial. Now, in a single step, this gave way to tall matai-totara-kahikatea forests in the eastern lowlands, and to rimu-rata-kamahi in the wetter western districts. As in the North Island some 4,000 years earlier, the transition took no more than a few centuries at any one site. Tall forest reoccupied the south in less than 1,000 years. As in the north, birds carrying fruit from isolated groves of trees into the surrounding grasslands may have been the key to this surprisingly rapid spread.

Although forests now dominated the lowlands, inland and upland districts tended to retain some of the original shrubland. Mountain toatoa, bog pine and other shrubs were more likely to be found at high altitudes, usually on poor sites. Thus dry, frosty, intermontane basins and drought-prone ridges were almost entirely in low forest-shrubland; midslope sites, with deeper, more fertile soils and more benign climates, would have had tall podocarps.

On the wetter, western side of the Southern Alps the vegetation sequence passed up from rimu-miro-rata-kamahi forest, through rata-kamahi forest, to subalpine low forest and shrubland with scattered mountain cedar.

By 9,500 years ago only central Otago remained free of any tall forest. There, shrublands, largely of *Myrsine divaricata* and small-leaved coprosmas, held sway. Only small pockets of forest — mostly groves of kowhai and isolated mountain toatoa, mountain totara and bog pine — grew within this, the driest district of New Zealand.

The interglacial peak : 10,000–7,000 years ago

About 14,000 years ago the sea level began to rise inexorably and by 12,000 years ago the North and South islands had separated once more. At around 9,000 years ago the sea level was still 30 metres below that of the present, and the present crenelated, rugged coastline was still well inland in many places. It was not until 6-7,000 years ago that the sea reached its present level, and it has fluctuated only slightly since then. The rise in sea level was a direct consequence of the melting of the northern ice caps and ice sheets. Much time elapsed between peak warming and the final high sea level because of the slow rate of melting and the vast amount of ice to be melted. New Zealand experienced its warmest, mildest conditions, therefore, long before the final disappearance of the global ice sheets and the consequent rise of the sea level to its present position.

Between 10,000 and 7,000 years ago New Zealand had its mildest, least seasonal, and perhaps warmest overall climates of the last interglacial-glacial cycle. It was during this time at the peak of the present interglacial that the climate became almost subtropical. However, it was not simply a matter of warmer temperatures, but a change in nearly all facets of the climate and ecology.

Perhaps the most striking botanical difference between then and the present was the relative scarcity

(Continued on page 101.)

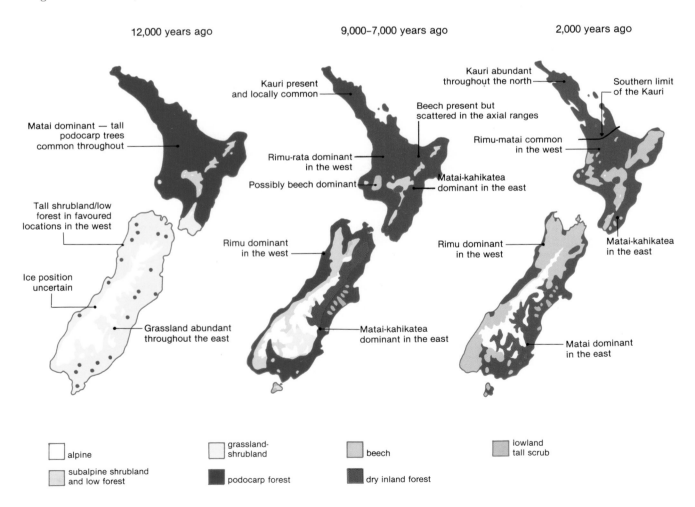

12,000 years ago

Matai dominant — tall podocarp trees common throughout

Tall shrubland/low forest in favoured locations in the west

Ice position uncertain

Grassland abundant throughout the east

9,000–7,000 years ago

Kauri present and locally common

Rimu-rata dominant in the west

Possibly beech dominant

Rimu dominant in the west

Matai-kahikatea dominant in the east

2,000 years ago

Kauri abundant throughout the north

Southern limit of the Kauri

Beech present but scattered in the axial ranges

Rimu-matai common in the west

Matai-kahikatea dominant in the east

Rimu dominant in the west

Matai-kahikatea in the east

Matai dominant in the east

alpine

subalpine shrubland and low forest

grassland-shrubland

podocarp forest

beech

dry inland forest

lowland tall scrub

THE BIRDS

AT the end of the last ice age, those birds that had survived the vicissitudes of the glacial winter spread with the expanding forests. Just how many species had succumbed to the harsh climate and habitat changes we do not know, but the low diversity of bird groups suggests that many extinctions had occurred. The passerines (song birds) seem to have suffered more than other groups from the loss of major tracts of forest during the glacial cycles, and many of the passerines in the fauna today are among our more recent immigrants. Apart from endemic 'wrens' (including the rifleman and rock wren), three species of wattlebird (huia, kokako, saddleback), two 'thrushes' and the yellowhead group, none of the present passerine species are likely to have arrived before the Pliocene. Most species in the earlier fauna had poor powers of flight, and most spent much of their time on or near the ground. The kokako and pigeon ate tree leaves, a niche usually filled by mammals. The passerines, like most of the fauna, laid the small clutches typical of species which are usually near the carrying capacity of the habitat. Some birds, such as the saddleback and snipe, could increase their clutch size when population density was low; most could not. During the Pleistocene when the climate deteriorated, and much later when predation on eggs and chicks increased after rats and other mammals were introduced, those birds laying small clutches were very vulnerable. Extinctions followed.

North Island brown kiwi.

Some of the older groups, then, did survive the Ice Age, and these, which had been part of the New Zealand avifauna for a very long time, had evolved under unique conditions. Apart from bats, there were no terrestrial mammals, and so 'mammal niches' were filled by birds. Flightlessness, gigantism, low clutch sizes, cryptic plumage patterns and nocturnal behaviour were common. Some species, such as the kakapo (*Strigops habroptilus*), exhibited all these traits; others just one or two. The kiwis even have body temperatures more like those of mammals than of birds.

Gigantism evolved most often in the herbivores.

Because plant materials have low food value and are difficult to digest, it is an advantage to be able to process large quantities at once. The larger the herbivore, the more efficient it can be. Large size is also an advantage because large animals use less energy per unit weight than small animals. For the moas, geese (*Cnemiornis*), takahe (*Porphyrio mantelli*) and kakapo, large size was a consequence of their diet. But becoming more efficient at exploiting a food source meant abandoning flight as a means of escape (and as a means of moving to new areas); this was possible only because there were no ground predators.

Not only large birds became flightless. Smaller birds of the forest floor, such as the snipe rail (*Capellirallus karamu*), did too; others, such as Finsch's duck (*Euryanas finschi*) and the New Zealand snipe (*Coenocorypha aucklandica*), could fly but rarely did. The rails and waterfowl were particularly likely to become flightless because their breast and wing bones do not develop until well after hatching. It is relatively easy for the process to be stopped entirely by a small genetic change. On the Chatham Islands, at least three species of rail became flightless: *Diaphorapteryx hawkinsi*, *Rallus modestus*, and *Rallus dieffenbachii*.

With the climatic warming, and as the surviving groups occupied new forest areas, new immigrants were carried from Australia by the West Wind Drift and occupied the forest edges and shrublands. In the postglacial forests, the forest floor had a rich fauna of frogs, lizards, snails and large insects, and many birds foraged there. In the North Island the snipe rail probed the litter and soil. A large coot and a rail similar to the Tasmanian native hen were common, and the snipe, which is now confined to subantarctic islands, was found throughout the mainland. Three species of wren, in addition to the rifleman and rock and bush wrens, hunted insects and spiders on the ground and tree trunks. The Stephens Island wren survived until 1894 on its island refuge, but lived then on both main islands. One of the others had very strong legs and may have been flightless; the third had a long, down-curved

ABOVE: *Although once abundant throughout New Zealand, fewer than 100 kakapo remain today. Formerly widespread through forested areas of the North and South Islands, the kakapo suffered severe decline because of predation by introduced mammals.* LEFT: *The extinct laughing owl.*

bill. A raven foraged along the shore and in more open forest, eating fruit, small animals and carrion. Native swans and pelicans lived on the large lakes and estuaries. Many species of ducks were abundant on the lakes, streams, swamps and coasts. The merganser, which survived until 1905 on the Auckland Islands, was then found throughout the main islands.

The most enigmatic bird in the lost fauna was the *Aptornis* or adzebill. Superficially rail-like, it was not closely related to any living bird. Flightless, it stood about 80 centimetres high and weighed up to 10 kilograms — the tiny wings useful only for display. Its neck was well muscled, and the huge, adze-shaped bill would have been wielded with considerable force. The bill may have been used to grub for roots, dig out burrows for tuataras or nestling seabirds, or tear open rotten logs for insect larvae. Adzebills seem to have been uncommon residents of the drier eastern forest of both islands. Like the dodo, it would have been very vulnerable to hunting and its remains have been found in Archaic Polynesian sites.

The large flightless goose *Cnemiornis* was similar in size to the adzebill, but its wings were larger. It grazed grasses and sedges along stream banks, in swamps, and in open forest and shrubland. Being flightless and short legged, *Cnemiornis* would not have moved far within its preferred habitat. The small flocks and family parties of *Cnemiornis* probably maintained areas of low sward, ideal habitat for rails and other small ground birds. These fat, sluggish birds would have been easy prey for the Polynesians and their dogs.

Another species of waterfowl was also a character-istic ground bird in New Zealand forests. Finsch's duck was a rather small bird which, although it could fly, probably spent much of its time on the ground, foraging for fruit, seeds and small invertebrates. It nested in caves, under overhangs, and probably under logs. It was very common in many places.

Although there were no mammalian predators, there were avian predators and some of the most spectacular predatory birds in the world hunted the birds of forest, wetlands and shores in New Zealand. The evolution of camouflage patterns and nocturnal habits of some birds is difficult to explain without the presence of these predators. The only nocturnal avian predators were the laughing owl (*Sceloglaux albifacies*), which fed on large insects, small birds and probably bats, and the owlet-nightjar (*Megaegotheles novaezealandiae*) which probably took large invertebrates, lizards and frogs.

The goshawk, a forest species and one of the largest of its genus, could have easily caught pigeons, kaka and takahe. Goshawks sit quietly on a concealed perch then dash after their prey, following it through the thickest vegetation and killing it in the air, or striking it on the ground. On the coasts of the Chatham Islands, and probably the mainland too, lived a huge sea eagle (*Haliaeetus australis*). Like its relative, the Steller's sea eagle of the north-west Pacific, this ate fish and carrion, but could vary its diet with penguins, the endemic sea duck, other seabirds and seal meat. The population was probably never large and the breeding birds would have been easily disturbed on their nests in rocks and cliffs.

In the mainland forests lived the largest, most

ABOVE: *The wrybill is an endemic species of the post-glacial period. An inhabitant of the braided riverbeds of Canterbury and Otago, it uses its unique curved bill to probe under riverbed stones for small fish and aquatic insects.* RIGHT: *The white heron has been an inhabitant of New Zealand's coastal and inland waterways for at least the last 4,000 years, although the depredations of hunters in the nineteenth century nearly wiped out the species in New Zealand.*

powerful eagle in the world. The largest female *Harpagornis moorei* or Haast's eagle weighed about 13 kilograms and its wings spanned 2.8 metres, but the usual weights would have been 9–10 kilograms for males and 10–12 kilograms for females. Despite its weight and size, the eagle flew strongly, at speeds up to 80 kilometres per hour. Its diet was large birds, from pigeons up to geese and adult moas. As the herbivores evolved large body size, apparently the eagle did too, allowing it to exploit a food resource reserved in other lands for the great cats. Perhaps the largest moas outgrew, as elephants do, the threat of predation, but the young of all species, and the adults of most, were vulnerable. Because the eagle could not soar, it must have hunted like other forest eagles, by perching high on a branch until suitable prey came within range and then diving on it at high speed. The impact, which could knock even the largest moas off their feet, was cushioned by powerful leg muscles. The 75-millimetre talons were then used to crush and pierce the neck and skull of the immobilised prey. The eagle and its mate could remain near the kill for several days because there was no larger predator to steal it. Like all eagles, *Harpagornis* also ate carrion and preyed on trapped animals when these were available: eagle remains have been found in swamps and caves, along with moa bones.

With a life span approaching 20 years, the eagles occupied, in pairs, territories of up to several hundred square kilometres. They were found mainly in the drier eastern forest during the Holocene, but were more widespread in the scattered forests and shrublands of the Late Otiran Glaciation (20,000–14,000 years ago). Capable of killing a human, *Harpagornis* succumbed to the environmental damage resulting from Polynesian colonisation. Its habitat was destroyed and food supply decimated and it became extinct several hundred years ago.

From the evidence we have, the postglacial avifauna of New Zealand was rich. There were large and small ground-dwelling herbivores, insectivores and omnivores. Penguins and other seabirds lived around the coasts, and petrels probably nested inland in vast colonies. With no mammalian predators on the ground, but avian predators in the trees, loss of flight was not a handicap, nor was great size. Birds could feed like cows or horses, and be nearly as big. Those species which had to live in the trees evolved good camouflage, those on the ground were cryptic, nocturnal, or both. The conditions allowed the evolution of a highly specialised avifauna, but one which was extremely vulnerable.

Today, New Zealand's forests are quiet, eerily so, and empty of animals compared to those of pre-human times. An amazing diversity and abundance of animal life flourished here, but most of the unique and vulnerable species were exterminated by hunting, habitat destruction and Polynesian rats and dogs. More than 40 per cent of the bird species breeding in New Zealand when Polynesians arrived are now extinct, and most of these had gone by the eighteenth century. Of the remainder, many are confined to tiny, windswept islands, marooned by the devastation on the mainland — the remnants of a lost fauna.

99

Before the arrival of humans 1,000 years ago, an exotic birdlife proliferated in New Zealand's forests and lakes. These included: (A) rails, (B) takahe, (C) the flightless goose (D) pelicans, (E) native swan, (F) moa, (G) the raven, and (H) Haast's eagle (Harpagornis moorei) — *the largest, most powerful eagle in the world.*

(Continued from page 96.)

of beech forest. There were small areas of beech — the ranges near Nelson and inland ranges east of Tongariro volcanoes are two such examples — but nearly everywhere else beech was scarce or absent. The great stretches of mountain beech and silver beech forests, which now follow the axial ranges from Fiordland to East Cape and clothe isolated peaks throughout both islands, did not exist. In their place grew a great variety of low forests and scrubland. In the drier ranges, or those areas with relatively warm summers, mountain toatoa, totara and bog pine dominated the subalpine zone. Wetter areas, with relatively cool cloudy summers, had a range of kamahi, rata, broadleaf or mixed low forest and tall shrubland giving way to mixed hardwood shrubland.

Rimu reached its greatest abundance at this time; pre-eminent on the west coast of the South Island, it was also much more abundant than at present throughout the western two-thirds of the North Island. It was only in the east, coastal south-east South Island and Stewart Island that rimu was uncommon.

Under the prevailing mild, equable climates of the

interglacial peak it is probable that animal populations reached their maximum size. Podocarp forests were at their maximum extent and they are extremely rich in food resources, especially fruit and nectar for birds. Nevertheless, there was some brake on populations as New Zealand was not entirely predator-free. Beside the harrier hawk and the bush falcon there were several other larger raptors including the giant *Harpagornis* eagle. However, except for the tuatara and some of the larger skinks and geckos, there were no terrestrial or climbing predators that could take birds and their eggs, and no predators at all which could hunt at night by smell. Under these circumstances, large, flightless, cryptic and nocturnal animals were favoured, and hence the proliferation in New Zealand of large, flightless birds, large ground-dwelling insects, and the abundance of lizards and terrestrial frogs. Animals which now have highly restricted ranges — for example, the takahe (one area of Fiordland), the kakapo (a few scattered South Island localities), the tuatara (offshore islands), the giant wetas and weevils (offshore islands, and mainland remnants) and the native frogs (isolated locations) — were once common throughout.

We can only guess at the difference which this abundance of animal life must have made to our forests, now so often gloomy and devoid of movement and sound. Tall podocarp forests must have seethed with activity from the upper canopy, with its copious nectar and fruit supplies attracting birds and insects but also dangerous avian predators, down to the forest floor with its multitude of large insects, and the scurrying and probing ground birds and reptiles which avidly fed on them. It will be impossible to understand the ecology of that which remains of our once luxuriant plant and animal life until much more is known about this lost prehistoric New Zealand.

Cooler climes: 7,000-1,000 years ago

Around 7,000 years ago the climate began to cool markedly — a trend which has continued, with small fluctuations, to the present. Ice advances started again, becoming general throughout most of the Southern Alps mountain chain 4,500 years ago. Glaciers have continued to retreat and advance down their valleys ever since, suggesting a cool but fluctuating climate. Summers became relatively warmer and winters cooler. Frostier, droughtier climates replaced the mild, humid conditions of the early postglacial.

The most striking botanical change was the expansion of beech from the small pockets in which it had survived the last glacial and the warm mild conditions of the early postglacial. Beech now began to expand in many directions in both the North and South islands, and continued to do so until as recently as 1,000 years ago. A combination of cooler climate, greater rainfall and more turbulent wind conditions assisted the beech in its explosive spread across the upland landscape. By 2,500 years ago the transformation of the subalpine regions was complete. In Fiordland mountain and silver beech occupied most of the upland areas, leaving podocarp-broadleaved forest only in the limited lowlands. Central Westland remained free of beech, but in north Westland and

ANDRIS APSE LTD

Dense southern beech forest, Bernard Burn River, Bligh Sound, Fiordland National Park.

Nelson, the beeches dominate the landscape, with podocarp-broadleaved forest prevailing only on favoured sites. In the North Island axial ranges beech either became greatly more common — as in the northern Ruahines — or spread from restricted sites to form continuous upland forests.

Beech made little or no headway in the fertile lowlands on the drier eastern side of the South Island which remained virtually unchanged in tall to low podocarp-broadleaved forest. However, inland, the driest regions of the central Otago Mckenzie Country were abruptly covered with a low forest, primarily of mountain toatoa, bog pine, mountain totara, kanuka and, at higher altitudes, silver beech. This dry, inland, low forest extended from central Otago northwards through north Otago-south Canterbury districts, under the shadow of the highest part of the Southern Alps and into the drier regions of north Canterbury and Marlborough.

Opinions differ as to why the beech spread so dramatically. Some point to its poorly dispersed, winged seeds and the trouble which it has in establishing itself under anything other than its own canopy. As well, its seeds are not attractive to birds, making bird transport unlikely. These features, it is claimed, would have led to a slow, progressive spread. That the beech did, however, spread so explosively, so dramatically, in both the North and South Islands suggests that the deteriorating climate must have played an important part in this change.

Equally startling changes were occurring in the lowland forests of the western North Island and north-western South Island. While beech was replacing podocarp-broadleaved shrublands and forest in upland areas, major changes were underway in moist lowland forests. Kauri, tanekaha, rewarewa and kaikawaka now began to assert themselves on hill slopes, ridges, and on lowland bog soils. *Quintinia* — a subcanopy tree with a distribution split between the northern North Island and north-western South Island — progressively increased as well. As these forest species — largely trees of poor, wet soils and dry ridges — spread, the species that had earlier dominated the landscape now began to retreat. Rimu gave ground to matai, totara and a host of broadleaved species. Climbing vines and treeferns became markedly less common, while hutu, which favoured mild, moist conditions, faded to near extinction over large areas of the North Island. Hutu remained abundant only in coastal areas of the west coast of the South Island. These changes continued in lowland forests until at least 2,000 years ago. Most of them can be related to the disturbance caused by increased winds, droughts and frosts.

And then between 2,500 and 1,500 years ago many parts of both the South and North Islands were devastated by fire. Huge conflagrations destroyed most of the dry forests in central Otago and the Mckenzie Basin. Similar fires on a smaller scale burnt forests within the mountain basins of south Canterbury. Fires may have also burnt wetland forests as far north as North Cape. Increasing westerly winds, as well as high summer radiation, may account for this unparalleled outbreak of fire in what had been for 7,000 years a largely fire-free environment.

103

A state of flux

We have followed the broad sweep of change which has transformed the landscapes of New Zealand since the last ice age. Despite the vast alterations to the size and shape of these islands and the dramatic fluctuations from bare open landscapes to full forest (and back to grassland in those areas where fire had broken out) there were apparently few or no extinctions. As the availability of habitat and the prevailing climates changed, the flora and fauna of a region expanded and contracted in response. Populations seem to have retreated to very small patches of habitat in which they have survived for thousands of years, and yet remained capable of explosively expanding to colonise large tracts of the landscape. Little information has been collected about population fluctuations of birds and insects, but we can reasonably assume that they waxed and waned in harmony with the vegetation that sustained them.

About 1,500 years ago, perhaps some 200-500 years before the arrival of humans, New Zealand was pre-eminently a country of tall forests. Only 10 per cent of the total land area lay above the alpine treeline. In southeastern South Island, extensive dry grasslands occupied central Otago and parts of surrounding districts. Treeless grasslands were common in the basins of the Southern Alps, the isolated frost hollows of the North Island, and on river beds and sand dunes throughout. However, even in predominantly grassed regions, shrubs were common, and patches of forest survived even in the most extensively burnt regions. Drier regions with poorer soils — such as the Canterbury Plains — appear to have had low forests of kanuka. Wherever the landscape was disturbed frequently — such as on sites close to rivers, on steep slopes and ridge tops — shrublands, low forests and regenerating forest were common.

True swamplands — those with standing water for much of the year — were relatively uncommon. In their place tall, multistoreyed swamp forests, stunted bog forests and shrublands grew on wet soils to deep peats. Rimu, kahikatea, pukatea and swamp maire were the main components of these forests. Manuka covered extensive areas of wetlands, particularly raised bogs in Southland and the Hamilton Basin. Montane bogs often had stunted cover of bog pine and mountain beech as well as shrubby covers of *Dracophyllum*, manuka and other species tolerant of acidic soils and high water tables.

Although New Zealand was densely vegetated, and perhaps 75-80 per cent covered with tall forest, it was still subject to violent change as the agents of destruction swept the landscape. It is perhaps best to describe the forests as being in dynamic equilibrium with the forces of destruction, rather than painting a picture of tall dense forests changing only slowly, tree by tree, generation by generation. Wind, earthquakes, vulcanism, rain and erosion constantly reworked the landscape and the forests.

Subtropical cyclones frequently sweep over New Zealand and bring with them high winds and heavy rain. In their wake they leave flattened forests — especially on exposed slopes — and thousands of slips. Mountainous or hilly regions with weak rocks are especially vulnerable to the passage of such storms, and inland valleys are often choked with rock debris resulting from the cloud bursts in upland catchments. Strong southerly gales, and westerly winds blowing over the main ranges can also extensively damage forests. Heavy rainfall may flood rivers, which may burst their banks or change course, obliterating forests or burying them under metres of gravel and silt.

Devastating earthquakes have struck at many places within the historic past. Violent earth movements often

Ruins of the Hazards' house at Wairoa after the Tarawera eruption, 1886.

RUINS OF Mᴿ HAZARDˢ HOUSE 33 C. SPENCER

give rise to extensive slipping and damming of rivers resulting in the complete destruction of forests. Some areas, such as the Southern Alps, which are undergoing rapid uplift, have been shaken many times, and earthquakes may be one of the major ways in which forests in these regions are rejuvenated.

Volcanoes are often thought of as having played a major role in shaping the vegetation of the central North Island. This is indeed true, but the effects are often somewhat different to what is popularly imagined, and the most dramatic effects are short-lived. Andesitic volcanoes — represented by the cone-building vents of Taranaki, Tongariro, Ngauruhoe and Ruapehu — generally have small-scale eruptions in which ash, blocks and cinders are distributed over a small area, and lava flows are confined to the body of the cone itself. Occasionally more violent gas eruptions occur, in which hot ash and gas avalanche down the flanks of the volcano, but usually only over fairly short distances of a few kilometres. Direct modification of the landscape is slight during any one eruption but, over time, the deposition of ash, and the collapse of cones in vast avalanches has built large aprons of volcanic debris called ring plains. The most spectacular example is the Taranaki ring plain which surrounds Mt Taranaki and adjacent extinct volcanic remnants.

The Tarawera eruption of June 1886 is the only documented example in New Zealand of a major volcanic event which affected tall vegetation. In the course of a violent eruption lasting some four hours, thick deposits of scoria fell within a radius of 16 kilometres north and south of the mountain. An explosive phase of activity threw a thick sheet of hot mud, ash and sand up to 24 kilometres to the north-east of the mountain.

Much of the Rotorua-Tarawera district was in shrubland-fernland before the eruption, with isolated stands of forest. Tall forest covered much of the lower flanks of the mountain, but the crests and domes of the summit were in shrubland and dwarf vegetation. How much damage was done to the vegetation depended very much on how close it was to the craters and whether hot, wet mud and sand fell in that area or scoria.

Close to the craters on the flanks of the mountain, the vegetation was totally destroyed in most locations by the thick accumulations of hot ash and debris. Scoria and rock fall alone had surprisingly little effect on the forests, even when up to 60 centimetres of debris fell through the canopy. Within a few years there was no sign of damage. Where the mud fell, the taller trees were completely stripped of their leaves and small branches, and the understorey shrubs buried. Low-growing vegetation outside of the forest patches disappeared entirely.

Forest recovered well from the hot mud and sand fall. Immediately after eruption the forests were reduced to stripped poles standing out of a wasteland of grey mud. Within a few months, with the coming of spring and summer, many apparently dead trees resprouted. In the previous scrub and fernlands, bracken began to force its way through the thick mud and sand. Four years later, although the tallest and slowest-growing trees had not recovered, many of the others had and were growing vigorously. Scrub and bracken once again blanketed the landscape.

Only on the flanks of the mountain where the destruction of forest was near complete, and the volcanic deposits deep, was succession back to tall forest slow. Although 14 years after the eruption little revegetation had taken place, 30 years later hardwood successions dominated by pohutukawa, rewarewa, kamahi and shrubby hardwoods were well advanced in some areas. Today, 100 years later, forest has reoccupied the flanks and is spreading into shrubland successions (often dominated by tutu) further up the side of the mountain. Regeneration has been slowest of all on the crests of the domes but, even here, bare ground and mat vegetation is giving way to taller shrubland vegetation.

The sorts of forest successions seen on Tarawera have been discovered in fossil deposits on the flanks of active andesitic volcanoes such as Mt Taranaki. From this fossil evidence, and Mt Tarawera, we can see that moderate-sized eruptions have their greatest and most lasting effects within only a few kilometres of the crater. Forests and shrublands recover very rapidly if they are simply showered with mud and lapilli, even if the initial scene appears to be one of complete devastation. In the long term, the ash and lapilli enriches the soil, and this is the most permanent effect of these eruptions.

Although andesitic and basaltic volcanoes erupt more frequently than rhyolitic volcanoes, it is the latter which in sheer volume of erupted material dominate the volcanic region of the central North Island. In the last 750,000 years of vulcanism in the central North Island, 12 to 16,000 cubic kilometres of volcanic rock has been erupted; 94 per cent of this is derived from rhyolitic eruptions. This would be enough to blanket the whole of present-day New Zealand with 50 metres of volcanic debris — the height of a 12-storey building.

Rhyolitic eruptions are often of enormous explosive force and pour out vast quantities of ash, pumice and hot gases in a single episode. Hot flows of gas and rock particles (pyroclastic flows) surge across the landscape leaving behind deposits up to 150 metres thick. If these deposits are sufficiently hot, the individual rock particles weld together to form a solid rock called ignimbrite. Over 25,000 square kilometres of the central North Island is covered with ignimbrite plateaus formed by numerous individual pyroclastic flows, often of immense size. The best preserved of these ignimbrites is the Mamaku, which erupted from the Rotorua Basin about 140,000 years ago and now covers an area of 3,000 square kilometres to the north-west of Rotorua. The total erupted volume of this huge eruption is estimated at about 300 cubic kilometres.

The quantity of volcanic material or magma withdrawn from under the rhyolitic vents is so large that the roof of the magma chamber often collapses and infills with water. Most of the large lakes of the central North Island — for instance, Taupo and Rotorua — have formed in this way.

The Taupo Pumice eruption of 1,800 years ago was one of the largest eruptions that has occurred anywhere in the world over the past 7,000 years. Indeed, such was its magnitude that it was recorded in the annals of Chinese historians who heard the blast and later observed the climatic changes it brought about. Today we know a great

105

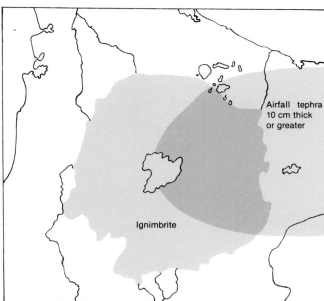

ABOVE: *The tephra fallout from the Taupo Pumice eruption of 1,800 years ago. Prevailing winds carried the ash over much of the eastern North Island.* LEFT: *A reconstruction of the scene 60 kilometres west of the centre of the Taupo eruption 1,800 years ago. During the 'ultraplinian' phase of the eruption a huge column of gas, ash and rock was flung 30–40 kilometres up. Preceding the flow, a shock wave radiated out from the centre flattening tall forest in its path. Here, wildlife, partially protected on the leeside of hills, tries to escape the impending disaster.*

deal about its effect on the vegetation and subsequent revegetation.

The eruption vent lies underwater in the northeastern sector of Lake Taupo. Lake Taupo was full at the time of the eruption and this gave rise to a complicated series of eruption phases as the water interacted with the hot (more than 1000°C) lava. The total duration of the eruption may have been as short as several days but is more likely to have lasted weeks or even months. However, the two eruptive phases which did the most damage to the surrounding vegetation lasted only a very short time.

After several eruptive episodes of relatively small size the 'ultraplinian' phase began. A huge column of hot gas, pumice, ash and rock particles was flung up to a height of 30-40 kilometres. In the course of an estimated six to 17 hours, more than 20 cubic kilometres of volcanic material erupted. Westerly winds carried the ash and pumice far to the east of the lake and, by the end of the ultraplinian phase, airfall pumice and ash deposits thicker than 10 centimetres coated some 30,000 square kilometres.

A sudden increase in the rate of the eruption of magma initiated the pyroclastic flows. In less than *seven* minutes some 30 cubic kilometres of volcanic material gushed from the vent, and at this point the eruptive column began to collapse. Huge avalanches of hot gas, pumice and rock surged from the base of the eruption column at speeds only a little slower than the speed of sound — in other words, at about 300 metres per second. At a distance of 20-25 kilometres from the vent the separate surges combined into one vast circular wave which stopped only when it ran out of material. As the flow sped from the vent area it incorporated air, and this increased the fluidity of the flow. The flow, lubricated by hot gas and many metres tall, ignored the topography of the surrounding landscape. Tall mountains in the vicinity of the lake were crossed by the flow, and only the massive bulk of the Tongariro volcanoes to the south deflected it.

The heat of the flow incinerated even the densest vegetation and the gases distilled from the wood were incorporated within it. A shock wave preceded the flow, and this flattened tall forests in its path. Right out to the limits of the pyroclastic flow, charcoal fragments and partially charcoalised trunks occur in the ignimbrite.

By the time the whole eruptive sequence was complete a roughly circular area of some 20,000 square kilometres was covered with thick ignimbrite. The very thickness of the ignimbrite in most areas close to the vent precluded the survival of any vegetation whatsoever. How-

ever, even as close as 20 kilometres to the vent, some forest must have survived in the lee of protective hills, perhaps as truncated stumps which later resprouted or as seeds in the soil. Towards the margins of the flow, forest survival must have been more common but, even so, only the odd tree or small patch of damaged bush would have been dotted here and there in a desolate, bare, eroding landscape.

Many have assumed that because of the nearly complete destruction of forest over such large areas forest regrowth and invasion after a rhyolitic eruption proceeds slowly. However, recent studies of the Taupo Pumice eruption of 1,800 years ago demonstrate that this is not true. There, bracken, scab-weeds, tutu and pioneering ferns, shrubs and herbs were quick to reinvade and within a few years the raw pumice was once again shielded from the weather by nearly complete vegetation cover. Fruiting shrubs attract birds, and a rich variety of secondary shrub and tree species became established, together with totara, matai, rimu and miro — the first representatives of the ultimate forest canopy. Within 300 years of the eruption, tall forest once again covered the landscape. It was not, however, the same as the pre-eruption forest. The layers of coarse pumice, sometimes metres thick, that blanketed the land replaced poorly drained soils starved of nutrients. These new soils favoured different trees. Matai and totara now dominated the forest canopy at the expense of rimu, beech and many of the hardwood species.

Not all the damage is restricted to areas directly affected by ground flows of hot gas and ash. Forests many kilometres from the eruption centre, receiving nothing

MATT McGLONE

more than a showering of a few centimetres of cold pumice ash, may often be disrupted by fire. A possible explanation is that the fallout of toxic chemicals in the eruption cloud kills foliage and vulnerable trees, giving rise to tracts of forests full of trees with dead, dry foliage. Under these circumstances fire is inevitable through lightning strikes, and repeated fire may result, which will not cease until the dead trees and foliage are replaced by regrowth.

Although the Taupo Pumice eruption was one of the largest of the last 20,000 years, it is but one of many which have created temporary clearances in the thick, dense postglacial forests of the central North Island. The most important ecological effects of these huge eruptions are not the dramatic and repeated destruction of so much forest but the constant rejuvenation of soils and forests.

We have talked about the constant churning over of vegetation, fauna and landscape by the external factors of wind, rain, fire, volcanoes and earthquakes. However, we should not exclude the relationship between indigenous fauna and vegetation which, unlike the other factors discussed, operates only in a very weakened fashion at present. Before the Polynesian and European destruction of perhaps 40 per cent of the indigenous birds, and the restriction to offshore islands of many once common birds, reptiles and insects, New Zealand forests had an almost unimaginably prolific animal life. We have seen how the abundance of fruit-eating birds may have assisted with the spread of forest after extensive destruction, thus promoting the self-healing properties which all forests have.

This was not the only role of birds. Many New Zealand birds in the absence of ground-dwelling mammals took on roles performed by mammals in most areas of the globe. For instance, the flightless ground-dwelling kiwi and weka, with their stout probing and thrusting beaks and strong legs are well adapted to seek out underground prey by probing, digging and scratching. Others, such as the kakapo, takahe and the moas fed largely on vegetable matter, occupying the role of browsing and grazing mammals. It is highly likely that these birds, capable of exploiting forests from ground-layer to high in the shrubby understorey, and of grazing and browsing above the treeline, had a marked effect on the vegetation.

Whether or not birds affected the vegetation as severely as the introduced mammals are capable of doing today is not clear. In dense, gloomy wet forests this seems unlikely. But, in open forests growing on nutrient-rich sites, it is entirely possible that their impact was rather heavy. Nevertheless, browsing by birds and mammals differs. Mammals can, for instance, strip bark off trees thereby killing them, but it is unlikely that the moa were capable of this. Sharp-hooved mammals compact and cut up the forest floor, doing far more damage than the broad, widespread feet of the birds.

We have seen how the biota of New Zealand evolved and reacted to innumerable changes of climate and topography over vast stretches of time. However, about 1,000 years ago an ecological influence, which was to dwarf anything that had gone before, made its first, fatal appearance. Humans had arrived.

LEFT: *Successive eruptions in the central North Island over the last few thousand years have mantled the surrounding area in a thick cover of unweathered debris, reducing much of the vegetation to scrub and grassland for brief periods.*

Today, the natural agents of destruction will sweep the landscape, constantly reworking its features. BELOW: *Storm damage to a southern beech forest, Arthur's pass, 1980.* RIGHT: *In the aftermath of the Inangahua earthquake in 1968, this huge slip blocked the Buller River.*

MATT McGLONE

GR

8. The human impact

In 1,000 years of human habitation the environment has been utterly transformed — its forests destroyed, while many of its animal species have vanished. Virtually nothing now remains of the original prehistoric ecology: a bitter legacy.

Pliocene		Pleistocene	Holocene

10,000 y.a.

THE land which was to become known as New Zealand had been separated from Gondwana for more than 80 million years when a new species, *Homo sapiens*, arrived for the first time. During this period of island isolation, a terrestrial flora and fauna, largely unique to New Zealand, had developed. Some of the species had evolved from ancestors which inhabited the original Gondwana landmass: others had arrived over the millennia by one means or another from other lands.

Below the treeline (which was controlled by the prevailing climate) the land was largely covered with forest or tall shrubs, the major exception to this being the area now called Central Otago. A high proportion of the plant species was endemic to New Zealand.

The terrestrial fauna was also highly endemic but lacking in variety, especially among the vertebrates. As far as we know, several small frogs and lizards, the unique tuatara and two bats were the sole land-dwelling representatives of the amphibians, reptiles and mammals. There was, however, an abundance of birds, although these too were limited in variety. Many of the birds had evolved for millions of years in a virtually predator-free environment and this was reflected in the high number of flightless or poorly flighted species.

The overall result of the isolation which led to this high degree of endemism was a terrestrial biota which was not only very specialised but also vulnerable to any sudden or marked changes of environment. One of the most striking features of this pre-human New Zealand fauna was that more than 90 per cent of it was confined strictly to the indigenous forest, without which it had little or no chance of survival.

The arrival of human beings marked the beginning of a series of unprecedented changes to the New Zealand environment, many of a nature and magnitude that had not been seen in the past. Certainly, New Zealand had been subjected to environmental changes previously — some gradual, some cataclysmic. There had been episodes of marine transgression and mountain-building, volcanism and glaciation that had markedly reduced the availability of a wide range of ecological niches, but, even so, most of the native plants and animals survived and thrived — or adapted and evolved into new and different forms. Man was to bring about more dramatic and drastic changes than had occurred during the last 80 million years and all in a few centuries — a mere moment of geological time.

Although it is nearly 130 years since Charles Darwin showed that man is a *part of* nature rather than *apart from* it, there is still a strong tendency to view the activities of the human species as 'unnatural', that is, as upsetting the 'balance of nature'. Quite apart from the arrogance of this assumption, in which people see themselves as playing a role of immeasurable power, it is not possible for humans, as a product of nature, to be *un*natural. Nor has there ever been a 'balance of nature'; nature is merely a convenient collective term to describe a number of processes which in themselves are always in a state of change. A human being is simply one kind of animal among the many thousands of animal and plant species which currently inhabit this planet, each competing with others for the best possible environment for its needs.

Of course, in singling out humans we are once again setting the human species apart. The reason for doing this is simply that this species has the potential to have an overwhelming effect on the environment, and has learned to manipulate it to a quite unprecedented degree. Man has the ability to create change in a way, and to such an extent, seen in no other species, and because of this there is justification for giving human-related changes separate consideration.

Nevertheless, it is important to remember that the environmental changes and competitive situations, such as predator-prey relationships, which resulted from the arrival of man in this country, should be considered to be as natural as those brought about by any other species moving into a new area. They were merely more far-reaching and extreme.

The Polynesian impact

We do not know exactly when *Homo sapiens* first arrived in New Zealand. Radiocarbon dating, the most modern and frequently used method of dating archaeological sites, is far better than anything used previously but nonetheless is not exact enough (particularly considering the relatively short time that people have been in New Zealand) to give more than an approximate arrival time. Nor can we be sure that dates have been obtained from the very earliest sites. But a reasonable estimate, based on all information available, is that *Homo sapiens* arrived in New Zealand about 1,000 years ago. Nevertheless, we know that these earliest comers were definitely Eastern Polynesians. A study of language similarities and artefacts (principally adze heads, harpoons, fish hooks and personal ornaments) from early sites of comparable age in New Zealand and East Polynesia suggests that the islands of the Marquesas and Society Groups were their most likely places of origin, with most recent archaeological work favouring the former.

We also know that the migrants brought with them other animal species — the Polynesian dog, *Canis familiaris*, and the Polynesian rat, *Rattus exulans* — as well as some plants — kumara, *Ipomoea batatas*, taro, *Colocasia antiquorum*, gourd, *Lagenaria siceraria*, and paper mulberry, *Broussonetia papyrifera*. As well, they carried with them their own tropical East Polynesian culture and technology, developed in and adapted to the environment from which they came. And as with humans everywhere this culture included the use of fire.

In their islands of origin the Polynesians had been accustomed to rely to a great extent on their domestic plants and animals which they took with them from place to place during island colonisation. They also made considerable use of marine resources, particularly fish and shellfish. New Zealand, on the other hand, presented a different range of non-domesticated plants and animals that could be utilised. Birds abounded in forests, around the coasts, and on the lakes and rivers; these included all the species of the flightless moas (Dinornithidae). There were, as well, extensive seal colonies, and both the sea and fresh water were rich in easily obtained fish and shellfish.

As a result, these early Polynesian colonisers initially

The journey to New Zealand was almost certainly made in a double canoe such as this one, recorded in use in the Pacific by Webber, an artist on Cook's third voyage, 1776–1780. Its overall length has been estimated at 29 metres and early reports indicated that some canoes could carry more than 250 people. (Drawing by Vivian Ward after Webber.)

adopted, or perhaps reverted to, what is popularly referred to as a 'hunter-gatherer' lifestyle. This was in marked contrast to the agriculturally based economy originally practised in their tropical island homes. Particularly during the period of early settlement, agriculture was not of great importance, being largely confined to the far North; a great deal of food, both plant and animal, was literally gathered from the surrounding abundance, while hunting, hitherto of little significance, became economically important.

The Polynesian dog and rat (kuri and kiore) also adapted well to the new conditions, spreading throughout the country. The dog remained to a great extent a human associate, but the rat moved into the forest in ever-increasing numbers.

Initial human population levels and rates of increase are largely a matter of conjecture. Nor do we know how they came; whether in a single large canoe or whether several groups arrived over a period of time. These initial migrants are thought to have settled here about 1,000 years ago. Within 200 years New Zealand had been completely explored, and an increasing population of humans was spread throughout the country. Sites such as that at the mouth of the Clarence River in Marlborough show that well-established communities of Polynesians were living here at least 750 years ago.

The same site also reveals the use of obsidian from which knives and scrapers were fashioned. Obsidian, a black volcanic glass, is of North Island origin — usually from Mayor Island in the Bay of Plenty. Its use in the South Island shows that early colonists must have travelled extensively in both islands.

But even at this early stage, changes to the pre-human environment had begun to occur: changes brought about by hunting and by the burning of the forest. Over the next few centuries the rate of those changes would accelerate, irreversibly imprinting the impact of man on the New Zealand environment.

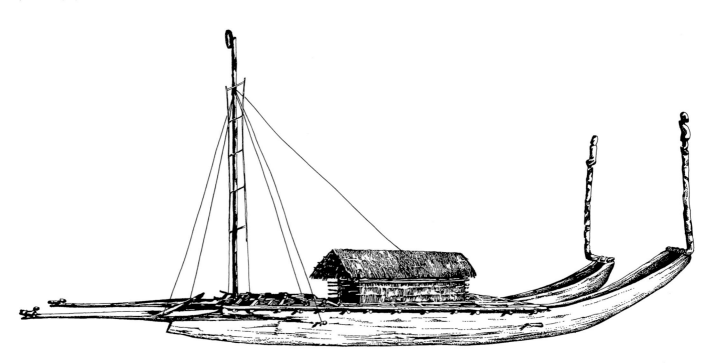

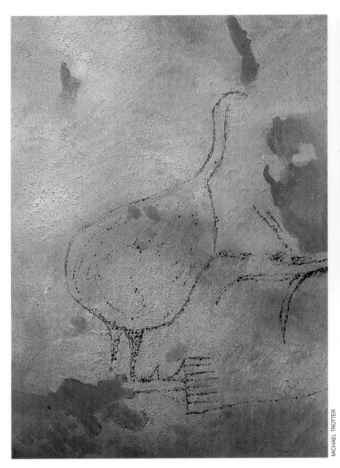

LEFT: *A charcoal and ochre drawing of a stylised moa executed on limestone in a South Canterbury rock shelter. Drawings such as these are at least 500 years old.* ABOVE: *Sub-fossil moa bones, Honeycomb Hill Caves.*

The extinction of the moas

In 1834 a trader, Joel Polack, when working in the North Island, came into possession of some bones, which he recognised as belonging to a large, flightless bird. In this way the moa was first recognised. In his book *New Zealand*, Polack wrote:

> *That a species of the emu, or a bird of the genus Struthio, formerly existed in the latter* [North] *island, I feel well assured, as several large fossil ossifications were shewn* [sic] *to me when I was residing in the vicinity of the East Cape . . . . The natives added that, in time long past . . . very large birds had existed, but the scarcity of animal food, as well as the easy method of entrapping them, had caused their extermination.*

When the first moa bone was sent to England, several years later, the great anatomist, Sir Richard Owen, also identified it as belonging to a large, flightless bird, to which he gave the name *Dinornis*, from the Greek meaning 'terrible bird'.

Since then, one of the greatest difficulties encountered in any attempt to study the moas and the causes of their demise has been the lack of reliable information about the living bird and its natural history. Its distribution, population, diet, reproduction rate and basic behaviour are still largely a matter of conjecture. To compound the problem, what evidence we have relating to moas at the time of their extinction, some 400–500 years ago, is almost wholly archaeological, that is, associated with human activity. Archaeological remains, largely from middens, yield even less evidence of moa biology and ecology than do so-called 'natural' deposits. However, we do know that when the first Polynesians arrived, all the known species of moa were still living, some in very large numbers, especially in the South Island. They represented a readily gathered, high-protein food source.

Archaeological sites in which direct evidence of moa hunting occurs are found all over New Zealand. Some are large, like those at the mouths of the Rakaia and Waitaki Rivers, covering several hectares. Other sites are small, like the oven excavated at Boltons Gully, Lake Pukaki, in 1969, which merely indicated an isolated 'kill'. It would be wrong, though, to assume that such sites reflect the distribution of moa populations of the time; they are affected by a variety of cultural and natural factors ranging from the favourability of the site for the preservation of remains to the amount of archaeological field research that has been done in any particular area. Many such moa hunter sites have been destroyed during the last century by European land development and also by curio hunters. Most of the early information comes from the east coast of the South Island.

Archaeological investigators of the last century left quite good records of the large quantities of moa bones which, at that time, could still be observed on sites. These sites provided evidence of 'former native feasts'. European agriculture, especially at the mouths of east coast South Island rivers, exposed 'acres of earth ovens' containing the bones of several different moa species — in some cases these bone deposits were so thick that they made it difficult to plough. Other descriptions tell of the ground 'white with great thick bones' and, at least at one site, at the mouth of the Shag River in Otago, wagonloads of moa bones were gathered and sent to the bone mills to be ground up to yield bone-flour fertiliser.

There was also evidence of apparent waste. In 1874 Julius von Haast, describing the moa hunter encampment at Shag Point, wrote of how:

> . . . *having such an enormous amount of game . . . they* [the occupants] *used only the main portion of each carcass for their meals . . . I was not a little astonished to excavate all the skulls in a perfect state, and, as the position of the vertebrae and of the tracheal rings lying along them proved, the whole portion of the upper neck had been thrown away, as of not sufficient value . . .*

This can only suggest an extravagant use of an easily obtainable food and similar evidence was found at other sites — particularly in the South Island.

The quantities of moa bones which had been left by the Polynesian hunters, and preserved by burial in the ground, quickly disintegrated on exposure to weathering when the land was ploughed. As a result of widespread European farm practices, subsequent investigators have not been able to repeat such spectacular discoveries, and some modern researchers have not fully appreciated the full extent of moa hunting activities, nor the economic importance of the moa to the early Maoris

— especially in the south. However, where recent systematic searches have been made to locate patches of undisturbed midden deposits on early sites, evidence of the plentiful use of moas for food has been found. Working at the Rakaia Mouth in 1967, Michael Trotter was able to repeat on a smaller scale the discovery by Julius von Haast 100 years before of a thick, moa bone midden on the same site.

The remains of moa eggs, too, were common on archaeological sites. Last century, descriptions suggested that a vast number of eggs must have been consumed as food. Walter Mantell's 1852 investigations at Awamoa, North Otago, clearly demonstrated their use; he recovered thousands of fragments of eggshell, which he measured by the gallon, noting: 'I know not how otherwise to describe the quantity.' Such practices must have had a deleterious effect on moa populations, especially as moas are believed to have had a very low reproduction rate, developed as a response to their original predator-free environment.

Nor were moa eggs used only as food. This became apparent at Wairau Bar in Marlborough. Here, in 1939, schoolboy Jim Eyles discovered an archaeological site which had been occupied by moa-hunter Maoris about 600 years ago. His initial discovery was of a moa-hunter burial complete with tools and ornaments, and, perhaps most exciting of all, a complete moa egg which had been drilled at one end to extract the contents.

Subsequent investigations showed that this was a large site on which the prehistoric Maori people had carried out a variety of activities. It was notable for its evidence of flaked stone tool technology, and the abundant

(Continued on page 117.)

The Canterbury Museum, Christchurch, 1872. Much of the early archaeological work on the moa during the nineteenth century was done by Julius von Haast, director of the museum. When the reconstructed moa skeletons were first displayed in museums, they were mounted at such an angle that the birds appeared taller than they actually were — perpetuating a fallacy that the birds always moved with their heads erect.

COURTESY CANTERBURY MUSEUM

THE TERRIBLE BIRD

IN the forests of New Zealand, without mammalian predators and isolated for more than 80 million years, the descendants of the original ratites had proliferated, developing in a distinctive way. The kiwis became the smallest of the group, all three species being nocturnal, insect-eating forest dwellers. The moas, although forest-dwelling, developed quite differently and in the virtual absence of any terrestrial mammals, had radiated into a variety of different forms and sizes, effectively filling a number of vacant niches in the environment. This process was aided by the range of the physical habitats available. As well, the division of the land into separate islands during the early Cenozoic had encouraged the development of separate species, each evolving its own distinct features.

No one is sure exactly how many true species of moas there were. The most popular classification in use during the past 40 years lists 29 species, but recent investigations suggest that there were more probably only about half that number. The difference is largely accounted for by the suggestion that moas were sexually dimorphic, that is, the males and females in single species were different size and shape, much as are today's domestic fowls. Nevertheless, we know that the smallest species was something under a metre in height; the largest, with neck extended, stood up to three metres, making it the tallest (although not the heaviest) bird that ever lived.

Similarly, no one has made any convincing estimate of their probable numbers. Certainly in the period immediately prior to the arrival of man about 1,000 years ago, moas existed in their hundreds of thousands throughout the country, but it is equally sure that some species were less prevalent than others. Some idea of their abundance can be obtained from Julius von Haast's descriptions of the deposits of moa bones located during swamp-draining operations at Glenmark, North Canterbury, in 1866. He described great masses of bones belonging to *all known species and to individuals of all sizes from the chick to the aged bird . . .* In places there were *. . . regular nests of moa bones . . . individuals of all sizes and ages*

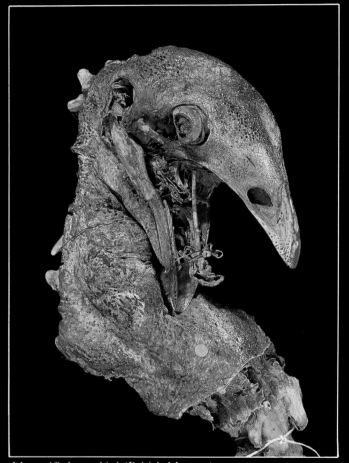

Mummified moa bird (British Museum).

lying together closely packed in spots 5 to 6 ft in diameter . . . I was sometimes enabled to extricate with some care the greate part of the same skeleton from the closely packed mass of bones.

Von Haast estimated that more than 1,000 birds had been trapped in springholes in one relatively smal swamp.

Their rate of reproduction is also largely a matte of conjecture although a low reproduction rate is usua in an environment which is predator free, as was th moa's until the arrival o man, and this is certainly so with the moa's closes living relative, the kiwi In some moa nesting sites found preserved under rock overhangs the nests seemed to have contained only one, or at the mos two, eggs. At Redcliffe Hill, overlooking the Rakaia River, 1,000 metres above sea leve and 75 kilometres inland a limestone outcrop had been used as a nesting shelter by several species of moas, and yielded egg shell of several differen colours, including a large portion of a single, unique, dark green egg which had not been incubated.

Moa eggs were usually cream coloured although some teal blue and light green shell has been found. Eggs of the larger species were up to 240 millimetres in length and the largest egg found to date has a capacity o 4,302 cubic centimetres or 90–100 average-sized hen's eggs. This enormous egg pierced at one end for use as a liquid container, was located at a moa-hunter burial at Kaikoura in 1857 by a workman at the Waiopuka Whaling Station of George Fyffe (Another ratite, the extinct *Aepyornis* of Malagasy, laid an egg of 9,720 cubic centimetres capacity — the equivalen of more than 200 hen's eggs!)

For many years it was believed that the moa's main food was grass, but it is now known that prior to moa extinction almost the whole of New Zealand was forested Recently, detailed examination has been made of the remains of several moas' last meals — these gizzard con tents were preserved in Pyramid Valley Swamp, North Canterbury, along with the bones of the birds that had been trapped there. The examination showed that the moas lived on woody twigs, leaves, fruits and seeds o

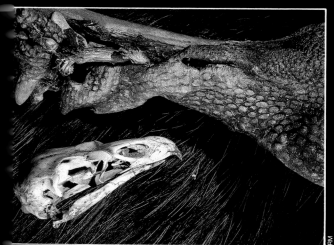

ABOVE: *The preserved leg and skin of a moa. The skull is that of a Haast's eagle* (Harpagornis moorei). RIGHT: *The compact and spiky branches of divaricating shrubs are believed by some scientists to have developed as a protective mechanism against browsing moas.*

forest trees, shrubs and vines. Among the plant remains in the gizzards were quantities of stones which had been swallowed by the birds to grind their food, thus aiding digestion. It has been suggested that New Zealand's divaricating plants (which make up 10 per cent of the country's woody flora) actually developed as a response to the pressures of moa browsing. Divaricating plants have a woody exterior with leaves on the inside, and a general tough springiness, which would have made them less palatable and may have afforded a measure of protection from the attention of moas.

There is no doubt that the moas' long legs and necks assisted them in their forest browsing habit, enabling them to reach high twigs and branches. However, modern studies show that for most of the time their necks and heads were carried forward in a more relaxed position. Early reconstructions tended to show the moa with a stiffly upright neck — undoubtedly in an effort to make it look as tall as possible.

Although these unique birds lived in great numbers throughout the country, they quickly succumbed once Polynesian man arrived in New Zealand about 1,000 years ago. Not only were they hunted as a good source of easily obtainable protein food, but their eggs, too, were taken and eaten. Moa bones were used to manufacture hunting weapons, fish hooks, and ornaments — while their eggs were also used as water containers. Dogs and rats, introduced by the Polynesians, also contributed to their decline.

However, the burning-off of the New Zealand forests by the Polynesians was probably of greatest importance in bringing about the moas' final extinction, destroying as it did both their habitat and food supply in a period of a few hundred years.

Radiocarbon dating of moa bones from middens on early archaeological sites indicates that the moas became extinct between 400–500 years ago. Despite suggestions that some of the smaller species might still survive in the remaining forests of South Westland or North-West Nelson, no one has been able to provide any proof that this is the case.

By the time Europeans arrived in New Zealand 200 years ago, the Maori people retained no real memories of the moa. From the time of Cook's first visit in 1769 to the late 1830s, there is no evidence of use of the word 'moa' to describe a bird, nor did any Maori report their former existence. When told by Europeans that moa bones derived from a giant bird, the Maoris believed it could fly and described it as both a swan and an eagle.

In the 150 years since then, numerous deposits of moa remains have been found throughout the country. The preserved bones of thousands of birds, both chicks and adults, have been located in swamps, with more in sinkholes, caves, sand dunes and loess. Some mummified material has turned up with skin and feathers attached, while eggshell and gizzard stones are quite common. However, the detailed study of moas has been largely neglected since last century and it is only in the last 10 years that renewed interest has been taken in one of New Zealand's most unique birds.

ABOVE: *The main moa-hunting areas of New Zealand.* LEFT: *Although researchers have suggested that there may have been up to 40 species of moa, modern research suggests that there were probably no more than a dozen, the difference largely accounted for by the possibility that the males and females of each species differed in both size and shape. This reconstruction depicts one of the smaller forms,* Anomalopteryx, *which, with neck extended, was probably little more than a metre in height.*

(Continued from page 113.)

kitchen middens which contained the remains of a variety of extinct birds — including the eagle, crow, swan and several species of moas.

A number of burials were located and these included, among the grave goods, at least six moa eggs, drilled at one end, and probably intended for carrying water. (In all, 15 eggs were found but the remainder were in too poor a condition to be able to establish clearly that they had been perforated.)

From such sites we now know that the early Maoris utilised moas for a variety of purposes. From the large leg bones they fashioned fish hooks, harpoon heads, necklace units, pendants and miscellaneous tools, while the skin and feathers were incorporated in clothing. And besides being eaten, the eggs were emptied so that the shells could be used as liquid containers. The location of moa egg 'bottles' interred with human burials at Wairau Bar and Kaikoura show that these were valued possessions.

After all the evidence has been examined, a clear picture emerges. When most moa-hunter sites were occupied — particularly the larger ones — moas were

COURTESY WILSON & HORTON LTD

plentiful (although some species less so than others). The Maoris hunted moas for food and robbed their nests. They were voracious and wasteful predators of moas and, although we have no direct evidence of it, it is almost certain that the introduced dogs and rats must have had a detrimental effect on these relatively defenceless birds.

Other ground-dwelling species were similarly affected. These included a large bird similar to a rail or woodhen, *Aptornis otidiformis* (as large as the smaller moas), and a flightless goose, *Cnemiornis calcitrans*. Several other flighted or poorly flighted species also died out during the Polynesian period, among them the giant eagle, *Harpagornis moorei*, which with the demise of the moas was deprived of its main food supply.

So far we have discussed only the effects of direct predation, but we cannot be sure if this in itself would have brought about the total extinction of the moa. The Maoris did something else much more damaging than direct hunting, because within 500 years of their arrival they had also destroyed a great part of the moa's habitat, and with it, its food supply. To do this, they used what was at that time probably their most powerful weapon — fire.

The burning-off of the forests

As early as the end of last century the early European settlers began to note that the remains of logs and charcoal could be found scattered over much of the unforested tussocklands of the Canterbury Plains and Central Otago. Similar evidence of fires destroying forests was also found

The extensive pits and terraces on One Tree Hill, Auckland, are evidence of the large size of the Maori settlements that once covered the volcanic cones of Auckland.

in Hawke's Bay. At first it was assumed that these were the result of 'natural fires' which had occurred some time in the distant past before the arrival of man. The failure of the forest to regenerate was thought to be due probably to the climatic changes since the last ice age.

Most early researchers were reluctant to ascribe the burning of such huge areas (almost half the original forest) to the activities of the Polynesians, and until about 25 years ago some refused to even recognise the past presence of such forest at all. In 1949 one scientist, Andrew Clark, discussing the existence of tussock grasslands in Canterbury, referred disparagingly to a 'hypothetical precedent forest'. Furthermore, an entire theory about the ecology of moas, also postulated in 1949, revolved around their being the 'equivalent of the hoofed stock now grazing our pastures'. In formulating this theory, Roger Duff of the Canterbury Museum suggested that the largest moa 'required as much grass per day as a bullock' (despite the fact that botanists had already identified the gizzard contents of moas from Pyramid Valley as consisting of the remains of forest plants). Such ideas have died very hard!

Even with the eventual general acceptance that forest or shrubland originally covered most of New Zealand below the treeline, arguments still raged as to the time and cause of its disappearance. However in the 1960s, with the advent of radiocarbon dating, it was shown that

118

forest destruction over almost the whole of the eastern South Island had occurred within the last 1,000 years, that is, within the era of Polynesian settlement. With the principal period of forest destruction now firmly placed within the period of early human occupation of New Zealand, it is now generally accepted that the early Maoris were responsible for these fires, although the reasons why such widespread destruction occurred are not clear.

One popular early theory held that the forest was deliberately burnt off as a stratagem when hunting moas — the fire driving them out so that they could be easily caught. However, this doesn't explain why the moas also died out in that half of the New Zealand forest not destroyed by fire. Some deliberate firing of forest areas was obviously carried out for a variety of reasons: to clear land for agriculture; to allow bracken, the source of fern root for food, to establish; to assist with cross-country travel; or to clear an area on which to build. None of these activities by themselves, however, reasonably accounts for the sheer magnitude of the area over which forest was destroyed. The most likely conclusion is that, although the fires were deliberately lit for whatever reason, they very easily got out of control. New Zealand forests, particularly in the drier, east coast, lowland regions, are especially vulnerable to fire — more so during times of drought. And in Canterbury an added danger must have been the hot, dry blustery nor'westers blowing down the mountain flanks and out over the plains. But just why forest failed to regenerate is not so clear. Obviously, some areas were deliberately re-fired periodically to keep them clear for specific purposes, but the greater part of the land simply reverted to tussock grassland or scrub or fern-lands. This is how the first Europeans found the country when they arrived to settle some centuries later.

Today, there is a tendency to be highly critical of European exploitation of the land, while praising the pre-European Maoris as conservationists who treated New Zealand with care and respect. While there is no doubt that the Maoris did have a great affinity for, and love of, the land, there is equally no doubt that they did substantially and irreversibly alter the pre-European environment. Besides burning off the forests and driving the moas and other bird species to extinction, they also seriously depleted the seal populations — especially in northern regions — while some shellfish and crayfish populations were so exploited that they never recovered. The tuatara also vanished from the main islands during the Polynesian era, either as a result of hunting for food or because of changes to its environment brought about by human activities.

Although Polynesian technology was not able to alter markedly the basic physiography of the land itself, the Maoris did bring about lasting changes to the soils in some areas as the result of their agricultural practices, most notably their kumara cultivation. These practices included the clearing of large stones, and the addition of a variety of materials aimed at improving the texture and fertility of certain soils. And in some areas such as at Wiri in Auckland, Palliser Bay in the Wairarapa and Clarence Valley in Marlborough, they left evidence of their agricultural activities in the form of dozens of low walls, which are still visible today, primarily constructed of stones cleared from the intervening plots of land.

They also left lasting monuments to their lifestyle in the form of terraced hill-top pa sites. Perhaps the best known are the volcanic cones of Auckland City, almost all showing the step-like modifications to their summits so typical of the hill-top pas of these people. In some places in the northern part of the North Island it is possible to stand on a height and see the summit of virtually every

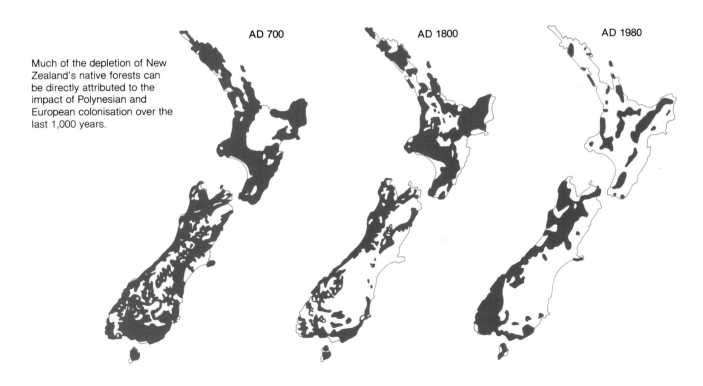

AD 700   AD 1800   AD 1980

Much of the depletion of New Zealand's native forests can be directly attributed to the impact of Polynesian and European colonisation over the last 1,000 years.

LEFT: *The red deer* (Cervus elaphus). *By 1900 at least 175 mammals and birds had been introduced into New Zealand, many by acclimatisation societies and sporting bodies keen to establish game animals.* ABOVE: *The wild pig* (Sus scrofa) *is descended from pigs released into the wild by Captain Cook and other early European voyagers plus domesticated escapees of the early years of settlement.*

hill within view modified by terracing. Such terracing will remain almost as long as the hills themselves.

So, after 800 years of Polynesian occupation it was a much-altered land that received the next wave of human occupation. But it was still a vulnerable land, a land of birds dependent upon the special environments to which they had adapted — and of unique plant communities, which, since the demise of the moas, had never felt the pressure of browsing animals.

The European impact

Although Abel Tasman had first sighted New Zealand in 1642, the earliest known Europeans to make any impact on New Zealand were James Cook and his men who first visited the country in 1769, at which time it has been estimated that there were some 100,000 Maoris living in the country. Over the next two centuries, Cook was followed by a succession of people, mostly of European origin: traders, sealers and whalers, missionaries, explorers, early settlers and, finally, from 1840, wave after wave of organised immigrants who arrived to take up permanent residence. The missionary Henry Williams estimated that in 1839 there were about 1,500 Europeans resident in New Zealand. By the time of the first official census, in 1851, there were 26,000; by 1936 the number had risen to 1½ million. Today the human population of New Zealand is about 3,300,000, of whom almost 90 per cent are of European origin.

Yet even before the beginning of the organised settlement of New Zealand in 1840, Europeans had already brought about many changes to the country; after 1840 these changes accelerated as the increasing European population placed more demands upon the environment.

On one hand there was the introduction, both intentional and accidental, of a wide variety of Northern Hemisphere plant and animal species. As well, there were groups of people deliberately exploiting — and thereby reducing — some elements of the indigenous biota by hunting, trade and collection for so-called scientific purposes. And there were European land-use practices which involved draining wetlands and burning off vast tracts of forest to an even greater extent than had been done by the Maori people. It is almost poignant to read today the accounts of some of these early settlers astonished at the scale of their own colossal destruction, how during a burn-off the sky would redden, then turn charcoal black, blocking out the sun for several days.

The first Europeans to introduce Northern Hemisphere species deliberately to New Zealand were those taking part in the expeditions of Cook and Marion du Fresne. They planted vegetable gardens in both the South and North Islands respectively, and Cook's men released pigs, goats and poultry. The introduction of the white potato almost immediately led to the increased clearing of land by the Maoris, particularly in the south where kumaras could not be grown because of the colder climate.

Although there is no known evidence, it is almost certain that the ship or black rat, *Rattus rattus*, escaped

ABOVE: *The Norway rat* (Rattus norvegicus), *the largest of the three rat species present in New Zealand. Like the ship rat* (Rattus rattus), *it has successfully colonised many of the offshore and outlying islands, where rat infestations have had a highly detrimental effect on native animal populations.* RIGHT: *Dead karaka forest caused by overgrazing.*

from the vessels of these early visitors, to be followed shortly afterwards by the brown or Norway rat, *R. norvegicus*. Both species rapidly increased in numbers to assume almost plague proportions. And at least one species of flea, probably *Pulex irritans*, arrived at this time.

Other early mammalian introductions were European dogs and cats — some of which quickly became feral. European dogs interbred with the Polynesian dog or kuri, which was not a hunter, and the resulting progeny formed wild packs that first menaced native birds — particularly the ground-dwelling species such as kakapo — and later the livestock of the settlers. Feral cats were an even greater enemy of native birds because of their ability to stalk and kill even flighted species.

Timber was soon recognised as a marketable product, being especially suitable for spars and masts. Particularly threatened were the great kauri forests of the northern North Island. Such a lucrative export trade developed around this timber that the kauri forests were decimated, and destruction continued at an even greater rate once the timber became much in demand for buildings within New Zealand.

New Zealand's marine mammals — seals and whales — were also victims of rapacious predation by Europeans. European sealing began in 1792 and continued indiscriminately for 30 years. During this period hundreds of thousands of fur seals were killed for their skins; a single ship, the *Favourite*, brought 60,000 skins from New Zealand to Sydney in 1806. As a result of this kind of hunting pressure the New Zealand populations of fur seals

were decimated, although open sealing seasons continued until 1946. The sealers were followed by whalers, initially working from large ocean-going ships, and then from shore stations. Their main prey was the larger whale species, principally the right, *Eubalaena australis*, the sperm, *Physeter macrocephalus*, and the humpback, *Megaptera novaeangliae*, which yielded enough oil to make the effort and danger worthwhile. As with the seals, the slaughter, including that of calves, was indiscriminate. Although by 1840 whaling had begun to decline around New Zealand, it was too late for at least one species. The right whales had gone and, except for a few isolated specimens, they are still gone.

But seals and whales were not the only large species to be affected by the advent of Europeans in New Zealand. The resident representatives of the genus *Homo*, the Polynesians, also suffered severe depletion of their numbers. There were two main causes of this. The first was the introduction of European diseases to which the Maoris had no resistance. Epidemics of such ailments as measles, which usually caused no more than a few weeks of discomfort for Europeans, often resulted in hundreds of deaths among the Maori population — both infant and adult.

All went well with the Maoris until 1848-49, when they were invaded by an epidemic of measles. This being an entirely new toxin . . . its effects were very severe; but the ravages of the disease were enhanced by their ignorance . . . they rushed into the creeks and into the sea to cool their fever-heated bodies, and died in large numbers, faster than their friends could bury them.

So wrote James Hay of Pigeon Bay whose family arrived in New Zealand in 1843.

But the land wars, the result of competition between the Europeans and the Maoris for occupation and ownership of land, also drastically reduced Maori numbers. Besides the direct casualties of fighting, wives and husbands were often separated for long periods with a resultant drop in the birth rate.

The Maoris, to a great extent dispossessed of their natural rural environment on tribal lands, suffered from problems of both health and morale. They did not adapt readily to a niche in either towns or suburbs. By the end of the nineteenth century the Polynesian population for the whole of New Zealand was less than 40,000 and the Maori was widely considered to be a 'vanishing race'. Only since the mid-1930s has there been any marked reversal of the situation, with a continuing high Maori birth rate complementing a fall in the mortality rate, as the Polynesian race in New Zealand has adapted to the prevailing conditions.

Nor were New Zealand's smaller terrestrial animals, especially the unique birds, immune from the detrimental attention of Europeans at a very early period. Throughout the nineteenth century, bird skins and mounted specimens were exchanged and sold in their hundreds all over the world to satisfy the needs of scientists, museums and collectors. As an example, in the late nineteenth century, Walter Buller, ornithologist and Fellow of the Royal Society, recorded shooting hundreds of pairs of the now extinct huia, including nesting females, to supply a ready market.

Mining accommodation at the Golden Cross Mine, Waitekauri, 1890s. Mining and forestry were extractive industries, dependent on non-renewable resources which by the end of the nineteenth century had been largely depleted.

COURTESY WAIHI MUSEUM

But it was not just in the removal, for whatever reason, of indigenous species of plants and animals that Europeans made an impact on the New Zealand biota. Like the Polynesians, they used fire to remove the native vegetation in order to use the land for their own purposes; this clearance included both mixed podocarp forest and also enormous areas of tussock grassland. Along with the destruction of the vegetation went the destruction of the fauna for which it was a habitat. It was during this period that species such as the native quail, *Coturnix novaezealandiae*, finally became extinct, while the range and number of many forest species as well was substantially reduced.

Almost as damaging as fire was the draining of great areas of wetlands for farming purposes. This change of ecology seriously affected the populations of freshwater birds and fish.

And still Europeans continued to introduce more foreign species of plants and animals to New Zealand. By 1900 at least 175 mammals and birds had been introduced into the country — many of which became established. Some of these — particularly the possums, deer and rabbits — were to have a devastating impact on the environment.

European land use

Most of the land cleared of indigenous vegetation by Europeans was converted to farmland — mainly pasture sown with introduced grasses and clovers. Initially, this was most successful in lowland areas but, as pressure for land became greater, more and more hill country was cleared, particularly in the North Island once aerial topdressing with artificial fertilizers became available after World War II.

One result of high country clearance, followed by stocking with sheep and subsequent overgrazing, was widespread erosion. In the South Island much of the tussock high country — fired almost yearly since the mid-nineteenth century, overgrazed by stock and over-run by sheep — was ravaged and reduced to barren, stony scree slopes with scabweed and the occasional stunted tussock clinging to the rock waste. Much the same happened in the North Island where the burn-offs had destroyed the protective mantle of vegetation, making the deceptively steep hill country prone to sheet wash, gullying and slumps. The established pattern of watersheds was altered, resulting in severe flooding in many regions — one of the most disastrous incidents

An aerial view of the Canterbury Plains. In little over 100 years European agricultural practices have utterly transformed the landscape.

being in 1938 when flash flooding in the Gisborne region killed 21 men when a public works camp by the Kopuawhara River was overwhelmed by floodwater. It was only in the 1940s, with the implementation of soil conservation and erosion schemes, that the rate of erosion and the consequent flooding abated — and with it one of the greatest threats to the economy the Europeans had developed.

On those slopes most prone to erosion plantations of the exotic pine, *Pinus radiata*, have often been planted. Their establishment has a two-fold purpose; apart from providing a protective mantle, binding the soil to the slopes, they are also an important economic resource. And nowhere is this more evident than in the central North Island where, unfortunately, little else grows — or can survive — in these vast mono-specific timberlands. They are certainly no substitute for the lost indigenous forests as an environment for the native fauna.

Nowhere, however, has the human impact been more complete than in the large cities, such as Auckland, where extensive tracts of land have been totally transformed into a matrix of tarsealed roads, motorways, dwellings and commercial premises. Unlike their Polynesian predecessors, Europeans do have the technology to alter markedly the physiography of the land. Road-making and mining are but two activities which can completely alter or destroy a feature of the physical landscape. In the Auckland area, for example, several volcanic cones have been totally removed by quarrying, while work such as the stabilisation of dunes or the construction of breakwaters and stopbanks, can halt or change the natural processes of sedimentation and erosion.

And extending from the towns and cities, with their industrial and business areas fringed with suburban housing, are the rural areas — farms and villages dotted with small agriculturally based businesses — and here and there a hydroelectric power station. All are interdependent, and all are influenced by the economic demands of the human population which created them. And as the whole structure changes in response to human demand, so too must the land which supports it.

It is 1,000 years since *Homo sapiens* arrived in New Zealand and in retrospect we can say their impact on the environment has been cataclysmic. The indigenous forest, which once covered most of the country, has been reduced to about 14 per cent of its original area; the native animals which were dependent on that forest have been reduced proportionately. Fire, flooding, erosion, drainage, pollution, economic exploitation and the introduction of a whole range of adventive plants and animals have all contributed to the changes which have occurred.

Charles Darwin, writing *On the Origin of Species*, in 1859, said:

> . . . *From the extraordinary manner in which European productions have recently spread over New Zealand, and have seized on places which must have been previously occupied, we may believe, if all the animals and plants of Great Britain were set free in New Zealand, that in the course of time a multitude of British forms would become thoroughly naturalised there, and would exterminate many of the natives.*

Sadly, his prescient warning has come true, although largely because of the effects of human activity. Today, the remnants of the original pre-human forest flora and fauna are largely confined to isolated pockets in reserves, or in the more remote areas of Westland and the offshore islands. And even on islands uninhabited by humans, the impact can be felt. When *Rattus rattus* jumps ship, the bird populations nesting in the crannies and rock outcrops of these islands are soon depleted, some lost. Virtually nowhere remains unchanged — such has been the effect of man's fatal appearance on these shores.

Select Bibliography and References

The following references are sources of general background material:

Archer, M. and G. Clayton (ed.), *Vertebrate Zoogeography and Evolution in Australasia*, Hesperian Press, Perth, 1984.

Cocks, L. R. M. (ed.), *The Evolving Earth*, British Museum (Natural History), London, 1981.

Halstead, L. B., *Hunting the Past*, Hamish Hamilton, London, 1982.

Imbrie, J. and K. P. Imbrie, *Ice Ages: Solving the Mystery*, Macmillan, London, 1979.

Laporte, L. F. *et al.*, *Evolution and the Fossil Record*, Scientific American Books (W. H. Freeman, San Francisco), 1978.

Press, F. and R. Siever, *Earth*, W. H. Freeman, San Francisco, 1974.

Smith, D. G. (ed.), *The Cambridge Encyclopedia of Earth Sciences*, Cambridge University Press, Cambridge, 1982.

Smith P. J. (ed.), *Hutchinson Encyclopedia of the Earth*, Hutchinson, London, 1985.

Thackray, J., *The Age of the Earth*, Institute of Geological Sciences, London, 1980.

Weiner, J., *Planet Earth*, Bantam Books, New York, 1986.

White, M., *The Greening of Gondwana*, Reed, Sydney, 1986.

Treatment of New Zealand topics is provided in:

Anderson, A., *When All the Moa Ovens Grew Cold*, Otago Heritage Books, Dunedin, 1983.

————, *Prodigious Birds: Moas and Moa-hunting in Prehistoric New Zealand*, Cambridge University Press, 1989.

Brazier, R., Keyes, I. W., and G. R. Stevens, *The Great New Zealand Fossil Book*, New Zealand Geological Survey, 1990.

Brewster, B., *Te Moa*, Nikau Press, 1987.

Cox, G., *Prehistoric Animals of New Zealand*, Collins, 1991.

————, *Dinosaurs of New Zealand*, Viking Pacific, 1992.

————, *The Stamp of the Dinosaur*, New Zealand Post, 1993.

Fleming, C. A., *The Geological History of New Zealand and its Life*, Auckland University Press, Auckland, 1979.

Forsyth, P. J., *A Beginner's Guide to New Zealand Rocks and Minerals*, Government Printer, Wellington, 1985.

Gage, M., *Legends in the Rocks: An Outline of New Zealand Geology*, Whitcoulls, Christchurch, 1980.

Hayward, B. W., *Trilobites, Dinosaurs and Moa Bones*, Bush Press, 1990.

————, and B. J. Gill, *Volcanoes and Giants*, Auckland Museum, 1994.

Homer, D. L. and L. Molloy, *The Fold of the Land*, Allen & Unwin, 1988.

King, C., *Immigrant Killers*, Otago University Press, Dunedin, 1984.

McCulloch, B., *No Moa*, Canterbury Museum, Christchurch, 1984.

McGlone, M. S., 'Plant Biogeography and the late Cenozoic history of New Zealand', *New Zealand Journal of Botany*, 23:723-749.

Martin, P. S. and R. G. Klein, *Quaternary Extinctions*, University of Arizona Press, Tuscon, 1984.

Morton, H., *The Whales Wake*, University of Otago Press, Dunedin, 1982.

Nicholls, J. L., 'Vulcanicity and indigenous vegetation in the Rotorua district', *Proceedings of the New Zealand Ecological Society*, 10:58-65.

Soons, J. M. and M. J. Selby, *Landforms of New Zealand*, Longman Paul, Auckland, 1982.

Stevens, G. R., *New Zealand Adrift: The Theory of Continental Drift in a New Zealand Setting*, A. H. & A. W. Reed, Wellington, 1980.

————, 'Southwest Pacific faunal biogeography in Mesozoic and Cenozoic times: a review', *Palaeogeography, Palaeoclimatology, Palaeoecology*, 31:153-196.

————, *Lands in Collision: Discovering New Zealand's Past Geography*, DSIR Information Series 161, Wellington, 1985.

————, 'The Nature and Timing of Biotic Links betweeen New Zealand and Antarctica in Mesozoic and early Cenozoic times', *Geological Society of London Special Publication*, 47:141- 66.

Suggate, R. P., Stevens, G. R. and M. T. Te Punga (eds), *The Geology of New Zealand*, Government Printer, Wellington, 1978.

Thornton, J., *Field Guide to New Zealand Geology: An Introduction to Rocks, Minerals and Fossils*, Reed Methuen, Auckland, 1985.

Wiffen, J., *Valley of the Dragons*, Random Century, 1991.

Williams, G. (ed.), *The Natural History of New Zealand*, A. H. & A. W. Reed, Wellington, 1973.

Wilson, C. J. N. and G. P. L. Walker, 'The Taupo eruption, New Zealand. I: General aspects', *Philosophical Transactions of the Royal Society of London*, A314:199-228.

Yarwood, V., 'The Hunt for New Zealand's Dinosaurs', *New Zealand Geographic*, 19:104-122, 1993.

Index